The Girl,
The Woman,
& The Crone.

A Journey of Love and Motherhood in Poetry

Front cover: Painting by Mary Lister, photo editing by Polly Walker.
ISBN: 9798336260755
Edited by: Polly Walker, Darkmoor Books
Copyright: Polly Walker & Mary Lister, 2024. All rights reserved.

Crone: [krəʊn] *noun*:

- "An older woman, mature and unfettered by the demands of love and motherhood, who performs a vital role in society, culture and family."
- "A woman or womxn of wisdom and experience"
- "One who sees with her heart."

Contents

Foreword 1

Prologue 3
    The Girl, The Woman, and The Crone 11
    Change: An Allegory 13

First Age: Birth 15
    Dreaming of Her 16
    The Tale of Roundly Bulge (A Sneak Preview) 17
    Once 18
    The Paradise Child 19
    Paradise in Bloom (Aged Two) 20
    The Toddler Queen 21
    Daughters of Copper Woman 22
    Kintsugi 24
    Silkie Ascending 26
    Sonnet to Simonetta: The Birth of Venus 27

Second Age: Girlhood 29
    Child of My Child 31
    Goldfinch Child 32
    Mummy, I Think I'm a Witch 33
    School Fat – A First Political Protest 35
    The Tragedy of Primrose Bear 36
    The Oster-Haza* (Easter Bunny) 37
    The Box of Delights 38
    A Princess with No Knickers 39
    Forged in Fire - Lessendrum 40
    Drawing in the Dark 41
    One World, Many Voices 42

Third Age: Youth & Love 43
    Listen to the Apple 45
    Fair Knights … A Courtly Love Poem 46
    The Changeling 47
    The Girl in a Veil 48

Feeling in Colour (Synaesthesia)	49
The Ballad of Mother and Daughter	50
Things You Are Not Supposed to Say	51
The Return of Spring	52
Warning Signs	53
Waves of Thought	54
The Click	55
Word Envy	56
Something Between	57
Wild Wounded Bear (Song)	59
Digging up My History (*Nem Santa, Nem Puta*)	60

Fourth Age: Maidenhood **63**

Questing Soul	65
The Link	66
Learning to Look and Listen	68
The Stillness (A Song)	69
The Negative Committee	70
On the You Beside Me	71
Do Not Miss a Day	72
I Cannot Keep Silence Anymore	73
On Brief Connections	74
Imaginary Argument	75
Porcelain Lady	77
Love Letter from an African Hotel Room	78
Widdershins	79
Scapa, 1945	80
The Transformation of a Winter Coat	81
Favourite Places (The Bookshop Song)	82
Lesions of Love	83
The Seven	84

Fifth Age: Motherhood **87**

Life Stirs in Me	88
Maiden to Mother: Waiting to be Rescued	89
This Darling Drudgery	91
Russian Doll	92
Seismic Shifts – on PTSD	93

    For Motherhood Sake, Create 94

    Love is Freedom 95

    Wide Open Spaces (The Sperm Bank Song) 96

    Nobody/The Invisible Woman 98

    I Did Everything Right, Didn't I? 99

    Other Men's Thoughts 101

    Hold Your Horses (A Song) 102

    Judith, by Klimt 103

    To Browning's Unknown Painter 104

Sixth Age: Crone **105**

    Reclaiming the Crone 107

    The Crone 108

    Sit Beside Me (to Rachel Lister) 109

    Mitochondrial Ball 111

    The Mystic 113

    How to Have Your Midlife-Crisis 114

    A Mermaid Comes Out on Her 60th Birthday 115

    My Grandmother's Hands 116

    The Window 118

    Rage 119

    My Muse's Ashes 120

    To a Modern Sculptor 121

    Villainous Villanelle 122

    The Cailleach 123

    Life Without Breath 124

    My Mother, Rachel 125

Seventh Age: Death **127**

    The Mother Ghost 128

    Lingers (the Unquiet Grave) 129

    The Mother-Daughter Turning Point 130

    Bedtime Stories 131

    The Cypress Fading 132

    Glass 133

    Two Dreams About My Mother 134

    It's Gone: The Inner Landscape of Dementia 136

    Forgetting Self, A Villanelle on Dementia 138

Fear No More	139
Listening to the Light	140
The Sleep Demon	141
Skipping Stones	142
The Carbon Cycle	143
Pass on a Little of What You Have Gleaned	144
Bound Wings	145
Child of Your Child – The Night is Behind Us	146
Death is a Garden	147

Suggestions for writers and groups 149
    Quick-fire warm-ups for groups or in pairs 149
    Writing prompts and inspiration 149

Foreword

"The Girl, The Woman, and The Crone: A Journey of Love and Motherhood in Poetry" weaves together the voices of three generations - a grandmother, a mother, and a daughter. The collection is grouped into the 'seven ages' from birth, childhood, puberty, through youth and love and finding independence, to motherhood, marriage, getting older and dying. In the first sections, the child's voice rings out with innocence and wonder, offering glimpses into the world through fresh eyes, curiosity and imagination, as she navigates the complexities of discovering her place in the world. The mother's voice emerges with a blend of tenderness and determination, capturing the joys and challenges of nurturing the next generation, whilst battling inner needs and ambitions. The poetry celebrates both the joys and the complexities of motherhood and daughterhood, acknowledge the sacrifices and struggles. In the last sections - Crone depicts the wisdom and beauty of growing older, the poems resonate with the strength that comes with age and taking up the mantle of matriarch within the family. The last chapter, on Death takes us through the painful grace of dying, saying goodbye to your mother and grandmother, and the love that lingers from beyond, treating it with affection and dignity.

Prologue

By Mary Lister

I wanted to compile this book with my daughter, to celebrate the life of my mother, and the wonderfully complex, sometimes fraught relationships between mothers and daughters. It has been a chance too, to explore my own daughter's thoughts on womanhood, so different from mine and of course, from my mother's generation.

I owe my love of poetry, song, and art to my mother Rachel. She grew up before the Second World War, in a remote but privileged house in Aberdeenshire, where her only entertainment was reading, painting, and making up dramas with her siblings. Instead of attending school, they were taught by a series of governesses, the last and best of whom introduced her to major poets and writers, as well as the great artists of the Renaissance. Mum could recite long passages from the works of Tennyson, Kipling, Shakespeare, Walter de la Mare, and many others, by heart. But when it came to her own poetry, she was extremely reticent.

When she was sixteen, she ran away from her then boarding school and went to art school in Dundee, and from there, signed on to the Women's Royal Naval Service (the Wrens), in 1940. She was posted to the Orkneys where there were plenty of Naval activities going on. It was an entirely new world to her, offering her the chance to interact with people from diverse backgrounds for the first time. Later, after the war, she went on to Chelsea Art School, which she loved. But when she met and married my father, that was the end of her career, as often happened to that war generation. Opportunities had opened up, only to snap shut. Then it was home and children, this "darling drudgery" as she refers to it in her poetry. Her 'career' then was to bring up three daughters, and later, as a devoted grandmother, bringing the family together, albeit with a firm hand, a true matriarch.

My happiest memories of my only surviving grandmother were her as a very white-haired old lady, playing the piano every evening at bedtime … to a very highly accomplished level. We would give her our requests and listen until we went to bed, lulled by Chopin and Beethoven. The keenest memories of my mother were of her reading or reciting poetry. In particular, when we had measles, she read us Tolkien's Lord of the Rings, illustrating the main characters like Galadriel, Bilbo Baggins, Frodo, and Aragorn. She even sent them to Tolkien, and we still have the lovely letter he sent back to her, which was very complimentary. I remember her humour and eccentricity too when she amused us with antics like dancing with knickers on her head in the kitchen and putting on funny voices when telling us stories. I also remember her shyness in company, something she taught us we must not be. We must not think of ourselves but be outward-looking and think of others. My only sadness about her later, was that she was too pusillanimous perhaps, to challenge the prejudices and inequalities of her class and background. Work was something her class and generation post-war were somewhat forbidden. The emphasis was on giving your children security and happiness, often at your own expense. But we were all three sent to a convent boarding school "to give us good manners" rather than an academic education… We already had good manners in bucketloads! She, meanwhile, sat at home all alone painting and writing poetry, never till now, to see the light of day. Later, my daughter's interest in poetry and her close bond with Rachel led to the discovery of her poetry, revealing a narrative of a woman torn between duty and domesticity and not realising the opportunities to fully channel her extraordinary talents. As a woman in the context of her generation, Rachel never thought of being taken seriously as a poet or artist. I, by contrast, have been able to make my living as both.

My mother's generation tasted a brief freedom because of the War, but lost it in the post-war fifties, and often returned to a stultifying domesticity, or poorly paid part-time employment. Mine is the Boomer generation, with free university education, the cultural revolution of the sixties, and the birth of the Women's Lib movement, we felt able to express our creativity, and freedom to be anything we wanted. We could dream and experiment, bring up children haphazardly, while working and living as we liked, barefooted, bra-burning or otherwise! Yes, we struggled and juggled all those things, and no doubt fell cheerfully between all the stools and chasms. It was hard work, but we could be free of class and rigid conventions. My generation had Women's Lib and the Pill. Writers like Simone de Beauvoir and Germaine Greer changed our narrative. We sought and found a new sexual freedom and self-determination. We maybe did not need to care so much about money and survival as this next generation now do. We were confident in the new caring state to look after our health and eventual old age. We were and are, the Boomer generation, now somewhat shaken by the new uncertainties and existential crises around the world.

My daughter's generation was different again, with many more opportunities for girls to excel in every field, including science and technology. More pressure perhaps, but for high-flying girls the sky was the limit, at least in theory, although glass ceilings still prevail. However, this also brought with it new pressures, i.e. to 'have it all' and 'be it all.' A Gen X woman is now somehow expected to be not only a perfect wife and mother at home, but also beautiful, high-flying, and successful in their own right. It is a huge challenge, and we have some incredible role models and success stories among women of all generations, to inspire us. To me, it seems an impossible Everest for every woman to juggle and climb. Social media also, whilst it can be enabling and groundbreaking, brings elements that are toxic and negative, pitting women against unrealistic ideals and creating a platform where they can be torn down with impunity. And whilst we, as women from white privilege experience these challenges, we acknowledge the even greater struggles of women from minorities, disadvantaged backgrounds, or from frankly misogynist cabals. What challenges and conflicts my mixed-race granddaughter will face as she finds her place and realises her dream to be a writer and performer, remain to be seen, but we hold hope things are slowly transforming for the better.

I encouraged my daughter Polly, to grab every opportunity that life could throw at her, and she certainly did that with both hands, albeit taking a different path to mine, opting to study science and getting a PhD in Virology. Ferociously adventurous, she travelled widely, often solo, in some wild and far-flung places, regaling us with stories of her journeys. One of those included getting caught up in a war in West Africa, which blew her mind open to the realities that many women and children experience in other parts of the world. When she returned from there she was changed - not traumatised but galvanised - and decided to return to Africa, and work in global health. After 18 years of this work, Polly's contribution has been through the lens of feminism, fighting for women's rights to education, equality, and indeed, to protect motherhood itself. From working with traditional midwives in West Africa to health workers in Sudan … Polly's work challenges gender narratives through public health. I'm in awe of the grit she has shown in the face of many challenges. Polly's own experience of marriage, however, only served to sharpen her vision of a gender-equal world. In contrast to me, marriage felt little more than a prison, preventing her from travel and aid work. Motherhood however has both transformed and grounded her. Although also torn between those equal but opposite callings of being a mother and pursuing her career, I have been able to step into that gap as a grandmother and literally 'hold the baby' whilst she does her thing!

For her generation, the existential question is *"Is there time to do it all, have it all?"* With dwindling childcare and limited provision for early years, a new dependency on grandmothers has arisen. The Grandmother has her moment once again. She is an essential and central person or rock, in the modern woman's toolbox! The Crone has come into her own, but she is still young and healthy, with all her teeth and faculties intact. No longer the toothless hag, mumbling and drooling. No longer the warty ancient bedraggled and demented sixty-year-old mutterer by the fireside. It is time to reclaim, and re-imagine the Crone as fit, glamourous, worldly-wise, well-travelled goddess, central to any family. She is seamlessly Girl, Woman, and Crone in one body and sound mind!

The Mother's role is primarily to nurture, protect and teach her children. To transmit culture, both of family, relationships, and community, but also of a wider sense of society and the world ... a moral and philosophical way of behaviour and thought, based on empathy, and understanding. But this too can be the essence of the conflict between mother and daughter as growing up, there is much protecting to be done! Daughters rightly perhaps, resist the strict boundaries of safety, and push the limits that their mothers impose. This does not only apply in the all-important, and fraught teenage years, where girls are easily flattered into unsafe relationships with others. But also in later womanhood, where the now older matriarch tries to impose the values of her generation onto a different zeitgeist, different in values and thinking. There is naturally a tension between generations. Often more intense in females, and perhaps because they need to grow away from their mothers and leave behind the values of their mother's generation, and the crone's wagging finger! Daughters often become mothers to their own mothers, as roles reverse in old age.

My own understanding of Feminism as I grew up, was that women artists, writers, and intellectuals had come into their own at last. But in all other walks of life, rights needed to be struggled and fought for, glass ceilings needed smashing. As a female performer, artist, and writer, I was given incredible opportunities and grants in a creative world where anything could happen, and the creative industries and arts were considered vital for social cohesion. In education, creativity was considered essential. Those days seem over now. Something my mother never could have dreamt of. But can my granddaughter dream of this in the future?

If I could talk to my younger self with hindsight, I would have told myself to be more confident in my creative powers, and more determined to take up the many opportunities I was given. I would advise my younger self to specialise more and diversify less. What I do applaud in my younger self, is my determination to help young people, particularly girls, to find their own unique voice, both in their writing and their creativity generally. Also, my decision to work in the toughest inner-city settings to reach children and young adults who did not have access to the arts. It was a privilege. If being a Crone means being a wise elder woman, and involves passing on culture, and filtering for a new age of the future, then I am happily a Crone. That being said, I have enjoyed every stage of womanhood, from girl through mother, and grandmother to crone myself, even though I know I can never achieve perfection … something all women beat themselves about with. What is the perfect woman? Does she exist, and would we like her anyway if we met her?

I was lucky to have an eccentric and wonderful mother, and two talented, funny and inspirational sisters. I am blessed to have a daughter who challenges, inspires, and encourages me, just as I hope to always support her in everything she endeavours, even now as a successful yet disabled woman, and mother. This book is for her, for my mother and my granddaughter, with huge love and affection. Above all, it is a celebration of all mothers and daughters, who form an immense human chain back through history. A chain of love and hope that carries the birth and renewal of the human race, with all its wars, conflicts, and suffering. We are pale but potent bearers of the flame, perhaps lit long ago by the Mother Goddess herself. And we are all Girl, Woman and Crone in our own lives.

Mary Lister

The Girl, The Woman, and The Crone

The girl in my mirror
stares knowingly back at me.
I look at her and see only what I see.
But she, from her glass world, sees me,
and over my shoulder
the little girl I was,
and the woman I am to be.

A little girl,
spares little time in her reflection -
she hurriedly yanks her ponytail straight,
and smudges marmite from her chin.
Without a trace of vanity
she scampers off to school.

The adolescent stares
more meaningfully now
and ponders over herself
like Narcissus in a pool.
She tries on expressions
to see if they fit
and critically examines breasts
for hopeful signs of growth.

The mirror now like a crystal ball
brings an image not yet reached by time.
A tall woman stands, pale and familiar,
fine lines drawn by laughter mark her brow.
Tired yet competent
she shepherds her children
into clothes, shoes, and buses
then sets off to work.

An old woman stands,
stares at the glass
her life, well-lived, her children gone.
She wonders where the time all went
and here she stands alone.
Her mind, unchained by hormones

now free to write her book,
as cronehood gives a freedom -
"This Darling Drudgery" * had took.

Dissolving into daydreams
the mirror turns from smoke to glass.
All of this, yet unwritten
of a future yet to be
But what this woman cannot see,
is that the girl, the woman, and the crone,
are all me.

Polly Walker, aged 13.

This Darling Drudgery was a direct quote from Rachel's poem about motherhood and marriage – see Fifth Age.

Change: An Allegory

It was midnight, on Midwinter Night. The old woman, Sarah, lit a candle and went to the oval mirror on its stand, muttering a song softly. She looked at her reflection. Yes, her face was lined with sorrow. But laughter too. She stood in her long nightdress, unpinned her long white hair, and combed it with a tortoiseshell comb. Then she turned her wedding ring three times on her gnarled fingers.

At her left shoulder a child appeared, a girl with long fair hair. At her right shoulder a woman appeared, with golden tresses down her back.

"Greetings to you, the little girl I was." Old Sarah said to her younger self. "And greetings to you, woman that I once became."

They greeted her in turn. "Greetings Old Sarah, that we will become."

Then they held hands. Girl, Woman, and Crone. "We are all one, all intermingled."

They pushed through the mirror and laid it down. It turned at once into a vast lake with no visible ending. Old Sarah threw the comb into its moonstone waters, and at once a ship appeared, drawn by a huge golden fish. All three stepped aboard, ready for the journey. They laid back on silk cushions and sipped ruby red cordial served in crystal cups by invisible hands.

"Once again we must change, but this time it is the final change." said Old Sarah.

"But which of us three has experienced the greatest change in our lifetime d'you think?" asked the younger woman.

"Surely it's me!" said the little girl. "After all I grew from a minute foetus into a little helpless baby, and then into a full person ... I had to learn language from babble, I had to learn survival, and numbers, and reading, and everything. I was a blank space, but I became a fully thinking human being. I learnt love, from being a baby, and the first tremulous feelings of the adolescent. That is the greatest change surely!"

Then, Sarah the younger woman spoke. "I carried you inside myself, that baby and girl you were, with all your wonder and dependency. But I lived through the greatest change, from child to lover, from mother to wanderer, poet and singer, and from family to friendships, to society, learning and experience. Mine was surely the greatest of changes a single human being can undertake."

"But what about you, grandmother, older version of myself? Apart from creaky old bones, what changes have you been through?" asked the girl.

"Yes, Old Sarah. Surely you are just us two, getting old and crumbling?" said Sarah, the young woman.

Old Sarah, Sarah the crone who carried inside her Sarah the woman and Sarah the child, went silent for a while. "The changes I have undergone may seem more about falling apart than metamorphosing or even adapting to the times. They are more about the shifting landscapes of understanding and enlightenment."

"Wisdom, d'you mean?" asked the girl. "I could have done with a bit of that. I grew too fast."

"Patience, forbearance? I needed that. I was always restless and longing for change and new horizons!" said Sarah the woman.

"But mine is the greatest change," said Old Sarah. "Because the greatest change any human can make is of course Death. Only I can take you both within me, beyond experience and memory. And that is my power, the only power left to me. But I must take you both with me – all together."

They stood then and bowed their heads, and held hands, as the ship took them across the borders of Change and beyond, in that moonstone lake that has no ending.

Mary Lister

First Age: Birth

In becoming a mother, few moments rival the discomfort and joy of carrying and giving birth to a child. Yet the relationship between mother and child starts long before the birth, and perhaps even before the conception. The desire, or imperative of motherhood is compelling and can sometimes feel as though we are called to become a mother, perhaps even to this specific child. Rachel often told the story of the night she conceived her third daughter, as in a dream seeing her "tapping at the window, asking to be let in". Which prompted her to wake up her husband and crack on with the conception. She also proudly told of conceiving her first daughter on the banks of Loch Ness during her honeymoon, but her middle daughter, Mary, was conceived on the overnight train to Luneburg (not even in the sleeping compartment!). Polly had a similar experience with her daughter, whom she dreamt of three years before her birth, and describes in 'Dreaming of Her', which many years later she recounted to her child who replied "Yes, I remember that. I was crying because I wanted you to be my mum".

So, our experience is that the bond starts even before a woman learns she is expecting, weaving together the threads of love, anticipation, and hope. As a mother-to-be nurtures the tiny life growing within her, she embarks on a profound transformation, both physically, emotionally, and mentally. Each fluttering kick and gentle hiccup serve as a reminder of the miracle taking shape beneath her heart. The journey of pregnancy, with its highs and lows, cravings, and discomforts, is a testament to the resilience and the awe-inspiring power of the female body.

The so-called miracle of childbirth cannot be much glorified in poetry – it is undoubtedly a messy business that marks a watershed moment after which nothing is the same. As Rachel would say "worst pain, soonest mended". Once you are holding your baby in your arms you are irrevocably re-formed as a person. Through sleepless nights, vomit, and milk stains an extraordinary bond between mother and daughter is forged in the crucible of love and nurtured with each passing day.

Dreaming of Her

You told me that we would have a child
and last night as we lay, heads touching
I dreamt her into existence.
Soft-skinned, wide-eyed,
curious about all things.
I stood amongst strangers
but feeling strangely absent.
I thought I heard a baby crying
I left the party and went to find her.

In my dream, I saw her bedroom,
vivid with colours and creatures -
the bedroom of a happy child.
But she was not there.
I entered the house of my grandparents
and wandered through undiscovered rooms.
It was here I found my daughter,
wet-eyed and frightened.

I felt a glowing need to comfort her -
I picked her up in my arms
her whole form melted into my hug,
her fuzzy hair on my neck.
When I woke, my arms were empty,
but the feeling of her lingered, far away, but real.
I knew then - I had met my daughter.
And from that moment
she had redefined
everything that followed after.

Polly Walker

It seems as though our children choose us.

The Tale of Roundly Bulge (A Sneak Preview)

I dreamed a baby, mine and roundly.
Proud I was of Softly Downy.
See the fussy faces coo me,
roughly touch my bulge and warn me:
"*Do this, do that*" and "*Don't eat that!*"
"*Don't stay out late*" and "*Don't tempt fate*" -
My bump my bump, I *cannot* wait!
So, rubbing bumply-bulge expectant,
politely usher from my kitchen,
faces cooing, gently, dearly
are all but vultures to me really.
I close the door and ... Breathe. And rub.
My roundly Bumply-Bulge, my tub
My gift: I *cannot* wait, I must unwrap you NOW!
No doctor, nurse, well-meaning man
shall see your face before I can.
So, lying restly on the bed,
I push my bump six weeks ahead
and all red-handedly I catch you,
exhilarant at my sneak preview.
And there you are – it's you, it's *you!*

I seen you, you smelled, you breathed you in
to re-acquaint you to my skin, touch my lips to furry head
So, kitten soft and mother cat we curl in bed.
Is mine, is mine, and no one else.
Just mine, just mine. Who else, who else?
Then through forgetful sleep, I wake me
shake me off, recuperate me
and naturally remember what it seems I happily forgot.
I dreamed a baby, soft and furry, inopportunely ... *far too early*.
But wait me in the dawn of ages
while I kill more time and turn more pages
and read my bedtime story-life
of dragons, princesses and knights.
Until the night becomes the dawn.
Until the Roundly Bulge is born.

Polly Walker

Once

Once, long ago
we made children, and sent them
like lanterns on paper boats.
to sail down the dark river.

Once, the current flowed calm
and they sailed luminous,
bobbing ahead of us
in flotillas of tiny flames.

Now, our old vessel
lets in water at our feet.
We lose sight of their voyages
in the moonlit path,

but hear the roar and swell ahead
where rivers must divide.
They whirl ahead, blurred points of light
lost to our fading eyes.

Mary Lister

The Paradise Child

Excitedly awaiting the birth of my first granddaughter, whose given name translates, beautifully, to "paradise".

Complex trade winds brought you here,
global games played out on beaches wove your ribbons of birth,
- and birdsong of migrating birds
sung you to us from West Africa.

Now you are here with us,
with a promise and a song of paradise,
paradise on your sucking lips,
and milk and honey of a promised land.

Say 'Ahhhhh!' Djenna. Show us your baby bird gape.
Let the juices flow. Wave your exquisite fingers,
and kick your little dancing legs.
Our milk and honey child, our bird of paradise!

Welcome to a new land, this new shore called 'life'.
Bring us Kora harp-notes and harmonies,
blown on gentle winds by the breath of ancient gods
from far away across your distant seas.

Mary Lister

Paradise in Bloom (Aged Two)

She stands at her marimba, pausing,
sticks in hand, to gaze through the window
at our little garden.
Her Brave New World.

Fluffy-haired and fluttering hands,
she hurries to collect tiny stones
to store in flowerpots,
like an Empress's treasure.

And when she hears a blackbird sing,
she stops to listen
because Heaven has opened
and sung its song.

She picks blue flowers
and delicately threads their stems through a yellow leaf -
A boat fit to carry
A tiny Queen of Paradise.
She is all joy
and the world is new again.

Mary Lister

The Toddler Queen

She commands me like a tiny queen
imperious from her cot,
reared on hind legs
in a fluffy ermined sleepsuit.
"Up!" she says and I am.
"Come!" she demands, and I do.
"Ook!" she points, and I look.
"Cuggle!" … and my arms are ready.
She is all curled up sucking noises
as she sleeps in our "Big bed",
snuffling and dreaming baby dreams
of "Bokkle" and "Mummy".
Then we are off "Down-tairs!"
"Mornin' Toys!" "Mornin' 'Body!" she calls
to the circle of bears, where she holds court.
Then she pours with, delicate precision, "tee"
into miniature china cups,
and hands one to me.
"Dink!" she commands, and I drink.
Her language is Baby-Survival Imperative.
She is all queen and benign tyrant
of tiny royal decree.
… and I am her willing, loving subject.
Her will is my command!

Mary Lister

Daughters of Copper Woman

This is a song I wrote inspired by "Daughters of Copper Woman" by Anne Cameron about a First Nations creation myth from British Colombia. Copper Woman, the first woman, became lonely, and blowing her nose into a shell, she accidentally created original man "Snot Boy". Snot Boy gives birth to many sons, who go out into the world creating all that is bad and evil. Copper woman, in a desperate attempt to save the World, creates twelve warrior daughters to be repeatedly incarnated into human beings in order to do battle against them. They can be incarnated in any form they choose, their souls will never die, and they may only be recognised by their green eyes. My grandmother and I both have green eyes, and a certain feistiness!

Please do not confuse all these déjà vues
with common sense coincidence, there's nothing to lose
in understanding or comprehending all the more
that nothing ever lives or dies, and we've all been here before.

So, I say *"Remember me? We were brothers in the war.*
Take your eyes off my breasts, look at me reborn.
I've been a mother and a soldier, a farmer and a queen
Come a little closer and you'll see my eyes are green…
They are still green."

Sitting in the dawn of ages I decided to be born a girl,
thinking it an interesting way to see the world.
I wouldn't change a thing, but everyone revolves around the simplest of things.

> Flesh is just a tiny vessel for a soul to swim in.
> Sex can't only fall into simply men and women.
> These containers come in all colours shapes and sizes
> but the beauty and integrity lie within.

Time is on my mind and here I sit and count the lines
on your face and memorise every little trace.
But I don't believe in age I know you cannot recreate an energy
that has been already made.
It can only change, and we can only change our forms.

Staring at my skin, heaven knows what lies within
the myriad of colours paints the world, allusion to a kin.
I know we don't speak the same tongue
but when I'm speaking in tongues to you
I know you'll understand me.

Yes, I'm young, or so my skin decides,
but if you taste my blood, it's like oak-aged wine.
We grow in seasons and the leaves must die,
but our roots take us back to the beginning of time.

> Flesh is such a tiny vessel for a soul to swim in
> There is no black and white, nor simply men and women
> Gender and sex are just an educated guess.
> I don't believe in time, it's such a transient thing

I'll see you again, some other colour your skin
some other gender again, I know,
old or young or black or white or ugly, handsome, fat or thin.
I know - I'll recognise you again.

Polly Walker

Kintsugi

I first felt you, tiny caterpillar
flipping inside your cocoon.
Goldfish flutters,
then I knew you were here.
You were a secret to the world I could not hide,
nestled in the quiet dark within me.

Two weeks past due, stubborn as the moon.
You were too cozy, cradled below my ribcage
burying your feet in my diaphragm
when you yawned and stretched.
I tried to shake you loose, walking -
each motion an incantation, summoning you.

Time twisted, stretched thin between contractions.
The skin of my belly, a landscape of cracked earth,
unzipped by your turning.
I traced the silvery fissures, rippled in rows,
I was a vessel, breaking and remaking itself,
a Kintsugian beauty.

Forty hours of slow-burning waves
rolling and pitching, each stronger than the last.
I swayed through them, music in the air,
breathing into the weight of waiting,
counting, counting …

Then, I was a vessel split wide,
the ground cracking open to release a river.
I bent, breathed, broke,
became a doorway between worlds,
each push an ancient rhythm,
the African winds behind me,
ancestors humming by my bedside.

You slipped into the world peacefully
wrapped in a winding cloth.
They checked you for imperfections
perceiving the blue birthmark on your spine,
a piece of sky tucked into your skin,
a kiss from another world.

Your hair, thick and coiled with the story of your roots,
your eyes—dark, knowing, already wise—
locked onto mine as if you remembered me.
You blinked once, "I told you so".

When they left us alone in the quiet,
they told me to dress you.
My hands fumbled with cloth, uncertain,
realising how unready I was for this moment
and all the rest to come.
Newborn am I - as a mother.

But your eyes, still locked onto mine,
blinking, recognition … wonder.
your lips found me like you'd done this a million times.
Goldfish mouth opening and closing,
tiny starfish fingers clutching air.
Gravity drawing us together.
Through instinct, I dressed you in my bloodstained skin.
Flesh on flesh.
You fed on me, and I felt the gold and silver
from my heart -
flowing gently into the fracture.

Polly Walker

Silkie Ascending

A dark glittering is my tale,
flipped and too quick to see,
out of the oil-dark water.
I am Silkie, Silver Queen
of the seal grey sea,
up from full fathom five
to flop on rocks, sending diamonds flying
over the lap-lapping of waves,
singing my eerie echoing seal-woman song.

I loosen my pelt, my wet speckled fur
and stand wholly woman, naked
under that half-rocking
ghost boat of the tilting Moon.
Kicking my flippers aside
I flex my toes,
and now with silken fingers
catch the rope rigging
of that twisting ladder to the Moon,
and climb from water through earth to air.

I am Queen of three elements now,
creature of myth,
as I float suspended in the upper ocean of the sky,
on a slither of moonlight for a ship.

Mary Lister

Sonnet to Simonetta: The Birth of Venus

Sorrow is here and beauty from the tomb
mingled with love, bending rebirth and death.
In this sad face, that in the gentle gloom
of early dawning gazes, while the breath
from lips of swiftly rushing zephyrs lifts.
The heavy hair that streams about her form,
and slow towards the shore the queer craft drifts
on seas that never can have known a storm.
Soft roses perfect lightly flutter down,
sweet petal-patterned robe her vestal holds,
gold every hair that ripples from her crown:
Lorenzo's leaves picked out in subtle golds.
Search that dead face, and seek to know her mind,
and you may see those dreaming eyes are blind.

Rachel Lister

Second Age: Girlhood

Childhood is a rich topic for poetry, filled with imagination and the unique way children see the world. During childhood, girls are learning how the world works, and about their place in their family, school and the world around them. It is an important stage for learning about boundaries and social relationships, and in which circumstances she can assert her own wants and needs, and when she has to bow to the opinion of her parents and peers.

For us, girlhood was when you discover stories, art and magical possibilities as well as your own autonomy within the parental framework. All three of us were quite vocal, confident and imaginative girls, full of feist and fun. We discovered the art of being naughty, and of how and when to state or assert your autonomy, as illustrated in the poem "School Fat" or the "Princess with No Knickers" which are prime examples of us showing our early-stage leadership skills! Such stories become the stuff of family legend as we laugh at the spirit of rebellion, exasperating to parents, but so vital for the child's development. I think that what the three of us share within this collection, is our sense of the extraordinary, our humour and the sense of purpose that we found during our childhoods. It is not lost on us that we lived very protected childhoods, which allowed us to dream and to imagine, and it's these stories we share with you now.

Child of My Child

Child of my child – butterfly
Psyche, Psyche, where do you fly?
Frail wings beating over the wild
Waves of the sea – *"Where to?"* I say,
"Over the foam to Norraway*, to Norraway"
"But don't you fear to fall in the drink?"
"Butterflies are tougher than you think."

Rachel Lister

*Norroway – an old word for Norway.

Goldfinch Child

To my granddaughter and all children locked in tiny flats during the lockdown in 2020, and their grandparents who miss them.

A goldfinch came and sang to me
from our little apple tree.
"Where is she, the Goldfinch Child?
Where is Djenna? Where is she?"

I whistled softly piping words
in the Language of the Birds,
"Djenna will return again
to love each Goldfinch, Robin, Wren.

But times have altered, time moves on.
Djenna sings a different song,
caged in a plagued city far away.
She'll come and sing another day."

Darker times will fade, must pass.
My Goldfinch will return at last,
run through the garden, free and wild -
my darling little Goldfinch Child!

Mary Lister

Mummy, I Think I'm a Witch

Mummy? Mummy, I think I'm a witch.
It's really making me worry.
I've inherited from the mother-lines-
something strange, something otherly.
I've felt this ever since then dear Mum,
and now I really need to know.
What's with all these birthmarks Mum,
was I burnt at the stake long ago?

Mummy, from the moment I could rhyme
I cooked spells up in your kitchen,
emulating as I could,
George's Marvellous Medicine.
Picking herbs and drying, crushing,
boiling things in cauldrons, singing.
Somehow, I think I'm knowing things …
or am I just remembering?

Mum, I speak to birds and cats,
make flowers into potions.
I give meaning to my stones and rocks,
I think I can sense their emotions!
I know where tree spirits live,
they've taught me how to fly,
they whispered where the fae-folk dwell
- and where to find enchanted fungi.
It's not that I mind being bound, Mum,
in a curious mystic tryst.
But the power of nature calls me, Mum!
Do all girls feel like this?

Mum, I confess, I persuaded my friend,
and together we spoke to the fairies.
We wrote in a journal we called "Witches Weekly"
and filled it with mystical recipes.
I pretended we were playing, Mum.
Just a game between girls and familiars
 – but if I'm being unnervingly honest
I felt magic move in my fingers.
It's not that I mind, if I'm truthful,
it's a rare and beautiful bliss.
But the hills and mountains are calling me, Mum!

Do all girls feel like this?

"My child, my green-eyed gypsy child.
Blessed of Brigid, Celtic myth.
You must learn to hide your magic,
to live in this world, and to fit.
But deep, deep down, you know thyself:
My wild-haired child, a witch."

"… And, yes, my dear … to some extent
all girls do feel like this!"

Polly Walker

School Fat – A First Political Protest

FAT. Cold mutton fat.
What could be worse than that?
Only the drainpipes in the Wednesday liver,
only the 'train-crash' on the breakfast plat.
Only the concrete porridge that we fed the school cat,
that laid it out stuffed-stupid on the mat.

And so, I sat. I wouldn't eat it, and I sat,
arms folded, and I sat and sat.
Long after the tapioca frogspawn had been cleared away,
long after the other children had lined up and left,
long after playtime, and I missed the playground chat,
long after the maths test, though I was glad of that –

But the end of school bell went too –and still I sat, I sat.
And nothing the dinner ladies or the teachers said
would make me eat that fat.
No threats or shouts or bullying or spat.
I sat it out and won at last, vive la brat!
No fat, no fat, no fat, and that was that.

Mary Lister

The Tragedy of Primrose Bear

My big bear had a flowery name
because he was pale yellow.
But even at that tender age
I checked; he <u>was</u> a fellow.
I feted him with cups of tea
and picnics out of doors,
All the toys sat listening
and gave him full applause.

Primrose would sing gruff-throated songs.
Primrose could do a dance.
With Roddy the Horse and Miaou the Cat
Primrose could pirouette and prance.
But one day Primrose disappeared
the toy cupboard lay bare.
The other animals searched with me
but Primrose wasn't there!

My mother - may she be forgiven –
when a *'CHARITY'* came to the door,
in a generous moment of heartless fun
given Primrose to *'The Paw'**
Since then, I've always hated *'The Paw'* –
I don't know who they are –
They kidnap bears, they tie them up
and force them into their car.

'The Paw' are to blame for all that's wrong
and terrible and bad.
I knew that as a fact since then
'The Paw' are evil and mad.
And if I'm slightly mad myself
and petulant and wild,
then blame the whole thing on my mum
who TRAUMATISED her child.

But Primrose – oh where did you go?
Does some child love you still?
Do you sit on someone else's bed,
and hug them when they're ill?
Do you still both dance and sing?
And make some other child grin?
Or have you gone to teddy hell
In *'The Paw's'* recycle bin?

Mary Lister

The Oster-Haza* (Easter Bunny)

I knew that giraffes were dangerous.
"Shut the door! There's a howling Giraffe!" the grownups said.
They could shape-shift, flatline into sly 2-D, under portals.
But the Oster Haza was a whole step up in terror.
A distant cousin of the Easter Bunny,
with horrid yellow checked trousers -
(Rupert Bear meets Struwwelpeter's Hare's Own Child**)

We brought him back with us from Germany.
Or so my father said.
Perhaps hanging on sneakily to the undercarriage,
or grappling with the back luggage rack
with bandy legs straddling behind him in the wind…
A hare that flies in the night?

Us cousins were shut into Granny's bedroom
while the Oster Haza laid his evil eggs around the garden.
My sister tried to peep through the curtain.
But I, aged 4, screamed.
If she saw him, he would stare back with glass eyes,
and that would be The End.

"You can come out children! The Oster Haza's been and gone."
We ran out to find enchanting little pink, green and gold eggs
hidden delicately in flowers, on leafy boughs.
We shared our shining treasures,
so precious in a time of rationing.
Maybe the Oster Haza was not as BEASTLY as I thought.
Much fluffier.

Mary Lister

*From the German, Osterhase.

The Box of Delights

I opened a book, a Pandora's box of thrilling delights,
spiralling upwards and outwards to new worlds.
The Wolves are running. I feel my hair stand up on end.
I am wolf ... I am cat, I am whom I want.
I am the glittering girl on a black mare with gold wings.
I enter an ancient picture frame
to meet a great-great-grandfather,
and travel to other worlds, long ago, aboard the Plunderer,
and just make it home in time for tea.

I am with Kay, my boy soulmate.
We slide along corridors, disguised as mice,
follow Herne the Hunter bounding through forests
on his sleigh drawn by unicorns.
I wear scarlet shoes to jump over water.
I meet the Punch and Judy man,
holding arcane secrets of magical power -
The Box of Delights.

I am transported, terrified, to the Wizard, Abner Brown,
encounter Sylvia Pouncer, my first brush with evil...
a governess turned bad.
Transmogrified, we sing with mermaids.
And always, the wolves are running, running, running.
My hair billowing behind me,
I must fly back inside my bed, heart racing,
and turn the torch off, beneath the bedclothes,
before Sylvia Daisy Pouncer turns me back
into a real child.

Mary Lister

This is about reading the Midnight Folk and The Box of Delights by John Masefield, aged seven.

A Princess with No Knickers

A feisty girl aged only three.
Attitude: "Don't mess with me!"
"Knickers? No way - can't be arsed.
I will kick them right off, fast!

Went to a party at the vicars.
Lifted high the frilly frock –
"I'm the Princess with no knickers!"
What a shock! Oh, what a shock…

"Polly, get your get your things all ready".
Get your coat on. Fetch your teddy."
Little Polly gave a nod.
"Who do you think you are? God?"

"I hate all buttons, please excuse,
I will not wear my buttoned shoes!"
She buried them beneath some shrubs.
We found them eaten up by grubs.

"The colour orange makes me nervous.
And brushing hair? For what purpose?
We aren't going to see the Queen!
You're just trying to be mean…"

Independent thinker – from the start,
Instinctively, straight from the heart:
Women should not do what they're told,
whether they are young or old!

Mary Lister

Forged in Fire - Lessendrum

A shock of fear ran through her eyes, her legs,
charging down the staircase.
Images bright, burning, imprinting on a four-year-old mind.
Her earliest memory - a house razed to the ground in flames.
Years later, faded like old photographs
showed maids jumping from the roof into blankets,
and her father, adrenaline-fuelled strength
tearing ancestral portraits from their walls
hurling them wildly out onto the grass below.
She recalls the running, shouting,
and in a matter of minutes,
all was consumed.

Lessendrum - the first house in Scotland to have electricity,
was ill-fated and defeated, bound by treachery.
A curse borne of arcane clan feudery,
pronounced by dastardly clan McCleod – a sworn enemy:
"*It started with a fire and thus shall it end*".
That three-year-old girl, wide-eyed, teddy in hand
watching her ancestral home descend.
As all was lost, they fled to another haunted highland place.
And as she grew, her childhood forged a spirit
alive with ghosts, curses, fire and legends.

Polly Walker

The first memories of Rachel Lister (née Rachel Murray-Bisset) were aged three, waking up in the clan home, Lessendrum, as it burnt to the ground in 1926. Later, she told a story of ancient treachery between the clans in which a Bisset had set fire to the castle of a sworn enemy and this was some magical vengeance. There is some debate about which clan it was that cursed us!

Drawing in the Dark

I learnt to draw in the dark.
Measles, and two speckled sisters lie,
curtains drawn tight against blindness. *
There is my mother, at our bedside,
magically drawing figures out of a stark white page,
while we watch her inkling strokes.

Oh, the alchemy of her 4Bs and 3Hs
to beckon Tolkien's orcs out of their Mordor shadows!
Galadriel, Lady of the Light, tall and elfin,
waves her wand to ward away the pencil,
but emerges second-sighted from her blurred penumbra.
And here is Aragorn, cross-hatched with 6Bs
out of leaden pencillings,
his hood just revealing piercing eyes,
two pools of black with two white spots left un-drawn.

How could these mere lead sticks
summon up dark forests with chiaroscuro shadows,
opening out on third, then fourth dimensions?
Sfumato rays of light glow from elfin windows,
or moonlit backlights on Black Riders.
(She could almost draw the sound of their hooves.)
Then, sunlight on Arwen's armour, or firelight from dark towers.

I took my pencil and drew a childish sun … with one blazing eye.
My first house was a dark tower.

Mary Lister

My mother sent her drawings to Tolkien in 1954, and he wrote back to say he liked them very much.

*It was thought that Measles caused blindness due to exposure to sunlight.

One World, Many Voices

I dreamed I was not dreaming ...
I saw a tree with wide branches,
like veins reaching up into the endless sky.
Its roots held the Earth at its feet -
the Earth with its blue waters,
its continents of many lands and many lives.
The breeze rustled in the branches with a soft whispering,
which was the sound of children.

They whispered messages to the birds:
"*Fly to many lands, telling of one world, many voices,
where children sing of peace they may never know.*"
And the birds flapped their wings
and carried their messages up into the sky.
They whispered to the fish in the deep sea:
"*Swim across oceans, telling of many tongues, one voice,
where children cry and fill the sea with tears.*"
And the fish swam in shimmering shoals,
carrying the message of tears across the wide oceans.

Then they whispered to the insects that toil in the earth:
"*Struggle on tiny legs across the lands and huge continents,
telling of one Earth, which is a family,
of many lands, with one heart and soul,
of work and toil which is forever,
of poverty which lives in the shadow of wealth,
of famine and hunger which is never satisfied.*"
And the insects scuttled away,
carrying momentous messages over tough terrains.

Then I heard in my dream, which was no dream,
an answering murmur from children across the world,
sweeping through the branches of the tree like a great wind:
"*Use your voices, sing of sorrow,
with one tongue speak of injustice.
Labour together to build a new world.
Burn bright as lanterns.
Light a flame for Humanity.
One world, one Family of Man,
one hope ... many children.*"

Mary Lister

Third Age: Youth & Love

Adolescence is the second time in human brain development where there is a massive and sudden reformation of neurons, which brings with it profound transformations and intricate explorations of identity and, of course, love and infatuation. For adolescent girls, this stage is a particularly poignant chapter, for all of us, as it was the first time in our lives where we felt the need to express ourselves through poetry and song – many of the offerings were written by us as teenagers in fact. We attempt to delve into the key issues that shape the experiences of girls as they navigate puberty, and that gut-wrenching rupture in which we pull away from our mother and father accompanied by the usual baffling adolescent conduct – door slamming, brooding etc. This stage is as inevitable as it is necessary, for a girl to gain autonomy and independence, and navigate peer relationships. And yet, it's a time of great vulnerability as well. Central to the adolescent experience is the exploration of romantic and sexual feelings, falling in love and awakening to their sexuality. With the onset of puberty comes a surge of hormones and newfound desires, ushering girls into a realm of romantic longing, infatuation, and intimacy. Yet, amidst the thrills of first crushes and budding romances, girls may also grapple with uncertainties, ranging from body image insecurities to navigating consent and healthy relationships. Moreover, the exploration of sexuality can be fraught with confusion, shame, and stigma, in societal contexts that perpetuate narrow expectations on gender and sexuality. Whether grappling with questions of sexual orientation, gender identity, or pressure to conform to heteronormative ideals, girls may find themselves wrestling with self-acceptance, belonging, and authenticity. These are some of the issues we have tried to address in this chapter, largely speaking from our own experiences.

Listen to the Apple

On pondering sexuality in puberty, inspired by "Oranges are Not the Only Fruit".

Listen to the apple.
The flesh.
The symbol.
The food of gods.
The fruit of Venus
and the corruption of Adam's wayward mate.
The flesh.
The symbol.
Listen to the apple.

"Bite me,
bite me,
and dream of being free.
Taste the bitter resentment of Eve
as her wedding day was written off as 'sin',
and for six thousand years became a scapegoat,
for this first, and fairest sex.
And long for a succulent ever-after taste,
in another, greener Eden,
where we are naked together,
wives and wives,
and the trees bear fruit only for the barren.
Bite me,
bite me,
and dream of being free."

Polly Walker

Fair Knights ... A Courtly Love Poem

Fair knights on snorting, snaffling steeds
underneath my tower,
first, perform me daring deeds
and I will throw you roses from my window-box-ed bower.
Bring me claw of Chimera,
and griffin-lard from Nineveh,
and newborn baby dragon down
from which to weave a wedding gown.
Then, aspicked hoof of unicorn,
Some diamonds of the cosmos' dawn
a phoenix egg to breakfast on,
a hydra's head ... or two ...
and if by then you're still not dead,
I'll swear to love you true!

We'll build a castle in the clouds,
beneath the setting sun.
And all day I will sing to you
of bygone kings, and things
that other bygone knights have done.
And I will rub your armour bright
with sunflower pads and nectarite,
bathe you in ambrosia dew,
and cook you wild sea serpent stew,
tickle you with peacock wings,
conceive a dynasty of kings,
knit you vests of gossamer thread,
and kiss you in a dahlia bed.
Yes! I will be your fairy wife,
in happy-ever-after life ... If you are not DEAD!

Mary Lister, as a teenager

The Changeling

From new moon to dark moon, she slipped away,
waning into darkness from the bright babe she was.
The first empty nest: our family bed.
Pulled then from my arms, while I lay sleeping.
No more her night-creeping, bear in hand.
No more terrors feigned just to stay beside me.
She lies alone, she sleeps and dreams, of what? Of whom?
She will not say, but buries deep
in a heart of hidden things, her treasures keep.

Once my babbling sprite, a river of words,
chattering with questions from dawn's first light.
Now she sits, a ghost at the feast,
her presence, absent, her chatter ceased.
Though 'she' is here, my babe is nowhere to be seen.
Now a fragile memory, a lucid dream.
Three times I call, hear myself repeat, repeat …
and met by silence, she sits, she scrolls, we barely eat.

This mummy's girl, *"those mirthful Fae hath
to the wet wild wood stole her away."*
No more touch, no more embrace.
"Don't touch my hair, my hands, my face!"
Once bright-eyed bairn, her fluttering giggles
with merry bubbles burst beneath my tickles.
Now, Ice Princess, warm blood run cold.
Inevitably this fated tale unfolds …
What cruel enchantment steals her heart?
What dark sorcery pulls us apart?
On the Threshold of Becoming,
I fear, I see, a seismic shift impending.

From moon to moon, I watch my daughter rise
to meet her fate of freedom, her mother now reviled.
I felt that cord a-rending, breaking.
I nursed my womb now splintered, aching.
To see my babe, now changeling child,
from my arms, the Fae have made her wild.
This fairy tale fractures, our hearts entwined,
a curse of independence, the spell is too unkind.

Polly Walker

The Girl in a Veil

A poem about girls being lured to join ISIS in 2015, based on the Lady of Shallot.

A shy girl waits by a bus stop
for a bus that will take her to a lover she has never met.
A passion only dreamt as yet, discovered on the Internet.
A dark veil and modest dress hide her youthful restlessness.
The heavy cloth obliterates her personal desires, and hates.
She's etiolated, a hopeful flower by the crushing monolithic weight
of family honour, religion, gender, fate.
All bricks that make her prison walls, from which she seeks escape.

Oh, and the threat of marriage to a cousin of an uncle's friend.
Some businessman, god-fearing and respectable.
But inside this dark impenetrable cage
in the secret silence of her homework room,
like a pool of light, or crystal ball that Circe conjured up,
or the cursed Lady of Shallot's dark mirror,
lies her laptop - always the dark connector
to arcane secrets, dangerous people and forbidden spaces.
Its blank lens, searches like Sauron's piercing eye,
and there in the dull chamber of her bedroom cell
she roams the world, hungry for life,
weaving her own dreams innocently
around the siren songs of the dark web.

The wedding looms. A man is chosen, a bridegroom fit
to chain her down and tame her bit by bit.
But now the dark mirror draws her
With an electronic Muezzin call to come -
"Come be a bride of warriors in a holy war!"
She sees her knight in armour, dressed and masked in black.
"A warrior fighting needs a warrior woman,
passionate and loyal riding at his back.
Come to me, come! Throw off the ennui of family control.
Fight for a glorious revolution,
behind some doomed boy-lover for a new heroic state!"
She leaves the laptop, leaves the loom,
She takes three steps across the room….
The bus has left, the girl has gone.

Mary Lister

Feeling in Colour (Synaesthesia)

Emotions are the colours of our lives.
Like a picture, mistakes cannot be rectified
And I think every tear, every smile, every frown
and all the thoughts I haven't written down,
are blended, shaded, like a picture.

And I think that every bruise
has contributed to my shades of blue.
The purples, greys and greens that merge into the ocean
where each alone is never seen
together make the strangest hue:
my own uniquely shaded blue.

The sunset: the colours of the heart,
and the crimson it bleeds when it is torn apart.
The scarlet of the flame, the fire, the fight
that burn and scorch and rage inside.
As it blazes, it consumes
then like the sunset, dissolves into the blue.

In the foreground: yellow flowers of bliss
golden ginger amity and breezy tenderness.
Violets shimmer pinkly in a heady spring of lust
and all passions spent untimely
are as petals in the dust.
Joy that blossoms and beams
is soon to wither, in deference to green.

And this is my green: the colour of my trees.
Of my freedom, my hope, and my integrity.
A verdant jade of wisdom, that searches, finds, redeems,
forever to Nature binds me,
to nurture me to evergreen.

It's a portrait, of a landscape
of everything I've thought or known or seen
blended, painted,
like a picture.

Polly Walker

Some women in our family are synaesthetic: we link numbers or letters with colours. I have emotion-colour interoception, so literally 'feel in colour'.

The Ballad of Mother and Daughter

The Ballad of Love between Mother and Daughter
is a tango of joy, confusion and pain.
Transcending the footwork of all that you've taught her,
an improvised discord drives slowly insane.
Electric connection … repulsion … restrain
Their stances are rigid, their eyes intersect.
With passion, one blood vibrates in their veins -
The Mother's steps certain: to fiercely protect.
Each move is a clash—pull, push and regain
as each loving gesture fails to connect.
Refusing all guidance, the daughter in vain
stamps her own rhythm: resist and reject.

At the heart of this battle is love and frustration
disharmony, synchrony alternate beats.
The Mother, her eyes filled with sweet desperation
the Daughter defiant, the object defeats.
She wants freedom and peace, wants your help (but resents it).
In growth and progression, a pattern repeats -
an insult, a nip, kick or punch, then repents it.
She flouts supervision, from advice, she retreats.
As fights are so costly, they're better prevented,
so passive aggression takes over the sway.
As words, now unspoken and discourse absented
what hangs in the ether, floats darkly alway.

Mother searches despondent "Am I really the villain?"
Daughter tearing her hair out – "Can't she just understand?"
Mother thinks each abuse means that she's a bad parent
Daughter thinks each restriction maliciously planned.
Mother bribes, begs, coerces, her ploys underhanded,
rules are abandoned, her threats are all hollow.
Daughter whines, screams and curses to get her demands met,
but neither can lead, neither willing to follow.
One day, all this rumpus turns back into music.
When weathered, the storm builds a shelter of trust.
Then settles the ashes, as Mother and Daughter -
dance the Ballad of Love forged through boom and bust.

Polly Walker

Things You Are Not Supposed to Say

A poem about learning love etiquette.

I like you.
I like you a lot.
I miss you.
I miss you already.
I feel you.
I feel like I know you.
I feel like I've known you forever.

These are the things you are not supposed to say.
These are the things that scare people away!
These are the words that should stay in your mouth.
There's a time and a place when they ought to come out.
There is an etiquette, custom and norm,
when taking somebody's brain bags by storm.
These little cards should stay in your hand,
spontaneous moments be cautiously planned.
For the fear of being foolish is stronger in most
than the passion of instinct and ardour of hope!

But the fact that you say them, it's taken as read -
as a sign of the things, you would like to have said
if you had read the rule book from cover to cover,
then tossed it and burnt it with the rage of a lover.
So, I'll not be offended if you break the rule,
and abandon your pride like a sweet hopeful fool.
If you reign in your reason, but dignity save -
when hunting an elephant ... you've got to be brave!
So, when you see the light shine in the eyes of another
you must know them, a friend, if a lover or brother ... and say:

I like you.
I like you a lot.
I miss you.
I miss you already.
I feel you.
I feel like I know you.
I feel like I've known you forever.

Polly Walker

The Return of Spring

The winter's long, the world is old
when will return the Age of Gold?

Dim in a laurel grove
stands the sweet Queen of Love.
Pensive her gaze
round her in company
youth, beauty, jollity
careless frivolity
dance in green haze.

Yet ah, too soon, too soon,
dark night overtook their noon.
Brief was their day.
First, she, young and fair
borne on her flower-strewn bier.
Then he, the debonair
stabbed foully, lay.

*L'hiver est passe, quand
reviendra-t-il, le temps?*

Rachel Lister

"Le Temps Revient" was the motto chosen by Lorenzo de Medici for the tournament at which Simonetta Vespucci was the Queen of Beauty embroidered on a banner designed by Verrochio was borne before them in the processions.

Warning Signs

Marooned upon the sofa,
draped languidly around his shoulders,
we bask before a flickering screen like sunburnt beached survivors.
Watching squint upon the far horizon for some communication
wave-like muffled radio hum - white noise to find a station.

He sends me silent signals down the wires of his intent to touch.
One stroke of neck or squeezing hand to say:
"*The sea is calm; the waves are rough.*"
In every movement, a subtle response
shows up concern at this - something hidden in my gesture
a duller radar might have missed.

"*Am I ok?*" I am ok. "*Am I ok?*" I am ok, over.
Then just as suddenly, I'm gone,
as would a rabbit in a headlamp lit before the storms begun.
In anticipated fear of a propensity to freeze and sprint from things
when required to be my tiny self before my monstrous feelings.

He unearths in me a hidden gift that's ancient in its loveliness.
The warning signs have whispered to me these few hours and less.
That each second of this absent-minded fingering of hands
has made me more a woman, and more of him a man.

Treating then with utmost care between two darkening sheets
a passionate cyclone, heavy rain pours down our great relief.
He buries himself supine amongst my tangled hair and breasts
like a child run headlong through the bounding foam
and settles now to rest.

Minutes pass and he is ready now to run again that shore
ready and now primed to run it stronger, faster than before.
And as the circling storms abate, we reshape ourselves in careless bends
one kiss released, then rumours crackle on the wire.
Heavens burst and let the tempest rise again.

Polly Walker

Waves of Thought

As deep within the ocean bed
the murmuring currents ebb and flow
so buried deep within my head
the waves of thought go to and fro.

Forever restless, never still
and seeking what they do not know.
Yet reaching onwards to the will
that drives the force that makes them go.

Relentlessly are driven on
and flooding towards destiny.
Ah, words, with what a benison
you lightly fall from them – not me.

Will it to me be also given
to reach the heights that others trod,
to lift mine eyes and glimpse the heaven,
to humbly touch the feet of God?

In all endeavour, there is some
of that which God gave freely down.
But ah, how short of it we come
and how we fail to reach the crown.

So, jewel-like, soft words to string
that palpitating on the lips
may linger as a lovely thing
that cannot lapse into eclipse.

Just for a little space, create
a mortal paradise alone,
and have no angel bar the gate,
nor awful thunders from the throne

But laughter in a sunny place,
and beauty in a world of pain,
and dream of peace and hope of grace
and all the years rolled back again.

Rachel Lister

The Click

When I meet you, if I meet you,
we will click like car doors
and laugh like old friends
and our hands will fall together searchlessly
and simply 'fit'.

When I write you, if I should write you
you will rush in the rhythm of my words
and feel them in your stomach and below.
So much so, you can almost taste me
and your heart will make a tiny flip.
You'll say to yourself *"that's it."*

When I read you, if I should get to read you,
I will understand implicitly
and listen to you wholly and humanly
and when I finish reading you over and over,
I will have digested every morsel
and this will have nourished me.

When we kiss, if we should kiss,
we will fill the world with blissful peace
tell a thousand silent stories
and conjure storms between our merging lips.
When we make love, when we do, finally
it will bear all the signposts of a homeward journey
unweaving all the webs and tangles
of our previous adventures,
our secret history.
We will stay in quiet awe of its simplicity
and say together: *"that's it."*
That's the click.

Polly Walker

Word Envy

Give not freely words of love
bestowed on *other* women,
if they to me could taste so sweet
that I should seek to steal them.

Tell me neither rhyme nor reason
of deep-sown seeds ungrown
and silence please, while your heart leaps,
I'd rather (not) hear it so.

Show not your pastel shades of love
and honey-scented words
take all those pinks and pretty flowers
give them to *other* girls.

But save for me the best of words
like "life" and "soul" and "freedom"
and I'll thumb through pages of you
then at my ease to read them.

To she and she serve kisses straight
from mouth of he that made them.
But give to *me*, a wholly written man
through secret prose reveal him.

For kisses end, and laughter fades
but page and ink are true.
So, couplet-rhyme and intertwine
thy manuscripted self with mine
then precious line by precious line
we'll render fiction true.

Polly Walker

Something Between

Whilst exploring maturer themes in love, this poem is a play on the words 'something between them' exploring the forces that pull and push you towards each other in forming a relationship, whilst also endeavouring to pull down the walls that one inevitably puts up for fear of being hurt.

There's something between us.
Something between a cunning smile and blatant innocence.
Something between stupidity, madness, and common sense
Something elusive, indescribable that bears passing resemblance
to something else we know but do not care to recollect.
We tread our well-trod footsteps, unpremeditated yet.

There's something between us:
Like smoke unravelling round us,
through us up and into deep inside of us.
Like winds that pull and beckon us to drift to the other side.
And we heave up our anchors and set sail to the unknown -
intoxicated by sensuality that rocks us to and fro.
So, ebb and flow the tides, of seas that lie
in between you and I.

But, there's something *in between* us:
The edges of a poorly drawn and faded map
delineate the boundaries between this side and that
on which you stand, and I can see you there and wave
yet only waves come crashing back.
Bearing messages in bottles - prayers of hope and aspiration,
demanding compensation for your chivalrous devotion
your attempts to cross the ocean that lies,
impassively, between you and I.

There's something *in the space between,*
perhaps not born of our endeavour
that such crumbling desire could never hope of breaking through.
An unspoken bastion of protection.
Legionaries of dejection man the battlements.
Here lies a bulwark of brick wall solidity
prepared to face the onslaught of your battering ram of kindness
and endure battalions of tumultuous affection.

Watch your words, like soldiers fall
as prayers to a burnt-out candle,
coins into an empty wishing well
and echo in the darkness
of the infinity of space that lies
in between you and I.

There's something in between us
that separates us from ourselves and from each other.
My cheerless lust for solitude keeps me at bay from ivy-armed lover.
A selfish disbelief in the synchrony of life,
the duality necessitated by the left and right halves of the mind.
The fear to split the chains that bind - soul to mind to body
repelling inner space from outer.
Yet fear of isolation compels me to break the spell,
to venture from and conquer.
What fear, what force, what dread in me
could thrust such impenetrable frontiers
between two adherent souls as these?
Nothing. Nothing but the simple sense of history
that tars the brushes time again
on the tortured canvases we stretch within
to hide the empty space that lies between you and I.

So, yes there's something between us:
A link, a chink, a chain, a wall, a rock, a sea,
a sky of dim-lit hope, a world of changing scenery,
A galaxy of emptiness, a universe of apathy,
to cross, to seek, to find me.

Polly Walker

Wild Wounded Bear (Song)

I've learned to be grateful, learning to wait
for the moment you answer the door.
My biggest vice is that I'm indecisive -
but I've made mistakes before.
I take my time to be ready
I may take months to be sure.
Once it's decided, I can't be divided.
What's all this struggle been for?
Hope is a half-open door.

You say that tragedy suits me,
so, I keep my whimsical thoughts to myself.
This drama queen, well she knows what you mean,
so, she'll leave you to love someone else.
Did you know there's a ghost in your kitchen?
Wild-haired gypsy dancer on your stairs?
As I dance down the hallway, I let the towel fall away
you never know that I'm there.
Hope is an unspoken prayer.

Ever since - before - I even met you,
oh, how I've known you.
I've seen more of you than I dare.
I'm strange and I'm cold but then
you lay me open.
some of us have things that we don't wish to share …
But I'm still the ghost in your kitchen
and I'm still gypsy-dancing on your stairs.
As I stand in your doorway,
and watch the walls fall away
that doesn't mean I'm not scared.
Because love is a wild wounded bear.
Love is a wild wounded bear.

Polly Walker

Digging up My History (*Nem Santa, Nem Puta*)

They're digging up my history, they're trying to find a piece of me.
They want my eggs for breakfast, they want my dirty laundry.
They want to bring me down a peg, to hang my head in shame.
They want my guts for garters, they want to ruin my name.
They're standing at the sidelines, calling names, and pointing fingers.
They're turning backs and whispering, this joyless bunch of mingers.

And all because of something, a curious event,
by skill-less charm and hapless luck, I kissed somebody's boyfriend.
They could not pin this one on me, for though I was a sinner,
t'was his own lies, the perjurer, that wrung him through the spinner!
So, dredging back in time, the gossips tried to find some mishaps
and failed to find much juiciness involving other chaps.
They should not give up hope poor dears, just dig a little deep
and proof of my moral decay will come up by the heap.
They've labelled me a saucy whore, but they don't know the half it.
So selflessly, I'll help them now … to find some mud to stick!

It's true, I was a Queen of Vice, resplendent former glory.
My sins are many, conquests great, and this here is my story.
A wild and feral furry child, by five, I roamed the mountains.
At six I dabbled witches' spells and boiled up things in cauldrons.
At seven, I was tomboy tough, knew swearwords, climbed up trees.
I teased the boys and made them cry; I threw cowpats at Brownies.
The queen of playground punk I was, my Bulldog Charge was regal.
The teachers spanked my bum red-raw before that became illegal.
By twelve, I'd grown a pair of tits confirming "I was cool" -
combined with roguish charm became most popular girl in school!
My talents then included, at thirteen, buying booze,
and holding pencils in my cleavage which kept the boys amused …

Our girls'-school days were packed with pranks,
my wicked ways prevailed.
We hid the chalk and stole the plugs.
We vandalised and blackmailed.
All my wayward impishness I learnt there by the tonne.
I learned that maths it rhymes with *laughs*, and kissing girls is fun.
Triumphant through my puberty, all naughtiness diverging
then launched attack upon the world with all my devilish daring.
This cat has lived a thousand lives, a dozen alter-egos.
I've slept on tables, danced on bars, and sprinted in stilettos.

I've grooved at techno warehouse raves.
I've tripped on magic mushrooms.
Danced naked at the Beltane Fire.
I've brought biltong through customs!
Smoked chillums in the Himalayas, bhang lassis in Calcutta.
I've done things in sacred springs I wouldn't care to utter.

I've hitchhiked round the Outback, jumped trains and boats and tractors.
I laughed once till I wet myself, I've changed my pants in taxis.
I've scraped through un-repentant: my sheer luck was alarming.
I've been arrested, twice, but was released for being charming.
I've dressed in corsets, stockings, wigs,
I've stripped down to my knickers,
and streaked across a cricket green - *that* shocked a bunch of vicars!
At naked hot tub parties, my appearances were many.
In fancy dress, I made a mess, for which I'm legendary!
I've had some fun and then some more with girls as well as boys.
I've had a spank, a bonk, a wank, I know the names of sex toys!

So, you see my gossiping girlies, while I've seen my share of scandal
there's not a lot I haven't done or much I couldn't handle.
So, shovel all the dirt you like, baptize me femme fatale.
The fact you talk of me at all can only make me smile.
For in these 30 years and more, I've lived it smooth and rough.
I've lived each second, fearing none, but not to live enough.
So, if you want to call me names, then try this one to spite me:
I am a goddamn lovely, saucy diva goddess-bitch
- So, bite me.

Polly Walker

This poem was written in retaliation to being gossiped about by a group of girls for something as harmless as a kiss: noting women tend to hold other women accountable for male infidelities. This archaic mindset is affirmed in the Portuguese adage that a woman should be "Santa na rua, puta na cama" – a saint in the street and a whore in bed. This poem is intended to help the reader embrace the concept "Nem santa, nem puta – sou mulher!" – neither saint nor whore, I am woman. My early life was full of adventure, liberation and fun – just as it should be. Freedom is only way to live.

Fourth Age: Maidenhood

Moving from adolescence to adulthood is fraught with uncertainties, yet it is also a period ripe with potential. For many, this is a time to explore passions, cultivate talents, and define identity on your own terms before the weight of societal expectations, or the responsibilities of marriage, motherhood and career begin to encroach. Central to this journey is the quest for independence—a determination to spread your wings and soar, unbound by cultural expectations. Young women now are very much claiming agency over their lives, but this was not the case two generations back, an anguish evident in some of Rachel's poems here. In the case of some of Polly's poems, she was prioritizing her career but also felt conflicted over the solitude that accompanied that choice, for example, Favourite Places and Love Letter from an African Hotel Room.

The path to independence is not without its obstacles. Deep-rooted insecurities ingrained social norms, and the fear of failure often loom large, casting shadows of doubt and apprehension. It is a journey fraught with moments of vulnerability, self-doubt, and uncertainty that require courage and resilience to overcome (e.g. The Negative Committee). Now, in the millennial generation, we can see our daughters and granddaughters taking bold strides, breaking barriers, challenging stereotypes, and defying expectations in this 'maidenhood' era of life, where our stages are set. This chapter delves into the terrain of self-discovery and trying to escape the shackles of insecurity in pursuit of our dreams. Love also emerges as a key theme moving from contradiction to agreement – with The Seven depicting the moment of finding the ideal love.

These poems are a mixture of each of us, finding ourselves, finding love and a home, or resisting stereotypes and carving out new paths.

Questing Soul

Behold the blood-red bitter spindle tree -
what other kind of words would fitter be?
To show the suddenness of scarlet bough
and break across the silence of the grey
and undisturbed stillness of the sky,
to scatter brightness on the brittle leaf
and shimmer all its greenness into gold?

So, into sudden uproar springs the pool
when skyward thrust the mallards from the weeds:
So sudden springs the seeker's questing soul
unto the fierce outpouring of its needs.

Rachel Lister

The Link

To Anthony Wynter Lister, Rachel's husband.

Picking up books at random,
roving the public libraries,
bearing like grain the volumes in sheaves
homewards for winnowing.
So much that is learned and wise to me,
is but chaff and stubble.
Suddenly comes the connection,
the one that catches the heartstrings.
The link: between the words and their meaning,
And between my hunger and need.
As between thee and me beloved,
as between thee and me.

So it is with the painters, scanning
those canvases, each a wonder.
It is the works of few that have it –
that pull, that draw that compels me.
Strong and strange it draws, the link that vital connection
understood by Raphael, vibrant to Lippi, Filipepi, and Fouquet.
So, with the poets too, but there the pattern is different.
Still, it is there, the link, the pull at the heart root.
The coming home to a welcome -
As between thee and me beloved,
as between thee and me

Long ago, I sat in the darkness
and saw the majesty of Egypt,
ancient temples and halls of the kings.
Heard their names, Karnak, Thebes, Abu Simbel
Hypostyle halls, the wonders of space regulated
columnar, trabeated, the words an incantation.
Saw first the pantheon's shape and learnt of the cunning
eye-deceiving ways of the Greeks
who sacrificed truth to perfection.
Triglyphs and metopes, orderly succeeding.
Entablature, architecture; so much half learnt and forgotten.
What was it then I felt, and since have groped for blindly?
A great excitement, delight in the seeing and learning.

The link; the finding of peace in communion
as between thee and me.

As between thee and me beloved,
no need for any heart-searching.
Questions of shall and shall not
or need of further debating.
Just that, the link, the connection.
The leaping across of the current
between two points and the safe holding
of what is most tenderly dear
and the full knowing
unavoided, heart-rooted link that is
between me and thee beloved
between thee and me.

Rachel Lister

Rachel went to Chelsea Art School to study Fine Art and Architecture but then left after meeting her husband Anthony.

Learning to Look and Listen

Learning to look and listen, intent on diverse opinions.
Seeing and learning and reading, the ways of life to discover.
What is the end and the answer
to all these questions and strivings?
Only to know oneself as the end and beginning of knowledge:
See in oneself the only consciousness of existence,
all outside this small circle of me-ness is land undiscovered.

Never can be more than surmised – expressed, defined by another,
even by one most beloved, most near, and yet how divided!
He too, alone from the beginning and solitary forever,
looks in my soul through his eyes as out of a curtainless window,
barred from each other by matter, our minds reach out to o'er come it.

Touch the intangible, reach the ungettable – ah, and we know it.
Yet in our end and division, that ultimate journey
to a further unknown, a darkness or truth unimagined,
Can these two lone and slight infinitesimal beings
meet and cling in the void and know each other, one spirit?

Rachel Lister

The Stillness (A Song)

The silence, there's no such silence.
Be still my beating heart.
Recover in the wake of violence
what your true motives are.
The stillness, there's no such stillness.
Be still my trembling heart.
Revalue in the light of illness
what your true motives are

> You falter and you surrender and
> it alters and it renders you weak and defenceless.
> Are all men equal to this?

Emotion, there's no such motion
you rock me to and fro.
You watched me so closely
can you bear to watch me go?
The silence, there's no such silence
as you drive me home,
but I'm still undecided what to hide and what to show

As I lay there, by the bonfire
Chilumba Beach, what a beautiful scene ...
and I'm asleep, it doesn't stop him as he
touches my stillness, with dirty fingers
lifts up my dress ...
to find that I'm more than a man,
I'm more than a man to this.
With a face full of blood and broken glass -
he'll never touch this ...

> You falter and you surrender and
> it alters and it renders you weak and defenceless.
> Are all men equal to this?

The silence, there's no such silence.
Be still my healing heart.
Recover in the wake of violence
what your true motives are.

Polly Walker

The Negative Committee

In the heart of every woman,
in the bowels of the Earth,
the Negative Committee sits
tearing all her soul to bits,
debating her lack of worth.

"*You are not fit for purpose!*"
these inner critics sneer.
"*You'll not amount to anything much.*"
"*You're hopeless, dull, and out of touch!*"
"*You are too ordinary, dear.*"

"*You are no academic!*"
"*An artist? No, you're not!*"
"*Can you call yourself a mother?
A proper mum? Just pull the other!*"
"*What a load of rot!*"

"*You're no writer, or a thinker.
How dare you dare to dream?
Your total life is built on stress,
your ugly mug's a minging mess,
and your ambitions are a scream …*"

They vote you out of all your hopes,
reduce your dreams to rags.
They thrash and bash and trash you down,
and try to drive you out of town,
with psychological handbags.

Women - do not heed their words.
Don't let them undermine and scoff.
Tell this committee in your head,
regretfully you wish them dead.
And tell them to "*F*ck off!*"

Mary Lister

On the You Beside Me

Over this year I have developed
an inseparable relationship
with an imaginary version of you.
He comes with me everywhere I go,
whenever I laugh, he laughs too.
When I sit alone at a coffee shop
he is sitting in front of me smiling.
When I sleep, his arms are around me
warm and unrestricting.
He is the 'You-beside-me'
He is my closest friend.
He does not criticise or chastise,
he is proud and tender.
Beside the 'You-beside-me'
You are a relative stranger.
With him I do not need to speak aloud
to let him know my mind,
nor to touch him to feel him near.
When You come and He is gone
I miss *Him*
when *You* are here.

Polly Walker

Do Not Miss a Day

Since I fell in love with you,
I do not miss a day to tell you so.
I love to tell you in the morning
when we roll towards each other
like blind baby kittens searching for nipples.
We find each other's mouths and kiss
greeting like old friends reunited.
I love to tell you in the evening
when we sink into each other's arms
letting the day seep out of our bodies
like the last sand from the hourglass.
And when we come together in the night-time
I have to stop myself from telling you every five seconds
that I see your pleasured face.
But I tell you over and over
with my lips and hands and curling toes.

You wrote to me once to say
"*Words are easily forgotten but work endures*"
and if that work is the building blocks of love
these words are simple maintenance
to prevent them from decay.
So, ever since I had these simple words in mind -
I do not miss a day.

Polly Walker

I Cannot Keep Silence Anymore

No, I cannot keep silence anymore!
Needs must I speak a little of my heart
that wails and beats and longs to have its say,
too soon to know just what it wants to speak.
Perhaps too late for rapture anymore,
but anyway, the wish to speak is there,
and waiting cannot always service bring
to those who know they have a song to sing
but do not know the way to set the air.
Though they have made their heart a treasure store
of all the magic that the longing seek
to lead them dazzled on a sunlit way.
New glories ever round about them start
and worlds of wonders stretch their eyes before.

Rachel Lister

On Brief Connections

In the comfortable darkness,
lit by a sparkling fireplace,
we sat like old friends or
long-lost travelling companions
and exchanged our stories
like Vikings once did.
Warmed by the glow of easy company
against the bleak backdrop
of each other's loneliness.
Weary travellers comforted
by a welcoming sofa of friendship.
These fleeting moments of quietness,
the sparkling jewel of connection
between two passing spirits.
Without even speaking of it
we understand
the real and transient value of this,
you and I.

Polly Walker

Imaginary Argument

I don't mind being alone, sometimes.
Sometimes, it's nice.
I'll come home from work, relax, unwind... And talk
To my imaginary lover,
who's had a very busy day
doing something exciting and important
which he tells me about
while waving his hands in the air.
He's so busy!
And yet he always seems to have time to write
beautiful imaginary poetry about
how crazy he is about me.

Then together,
and sometimes with our clothes on
we cook imaginary food that we pretend to eat and it's delicious,
and feed our imaginary cats the rest.
Then see imaginary friends,
who love us cos we're so funny and charming
and sometimes we stay home and draw out plots for
our imaginary books we are writing which are *really* good.
We paint pictures on huge canvases in our studio,
or sometimes just build big shapes out of wire and wood
whatever imaginary things we happen to have at hand.
We spend forever in our imaginary garden
where everything just grows
and the sun is always shining ...
That's where we go to plan our next adventures.
And that's how crazy we are about us.

But then we're tired, and I've got an imaginary headache,
so he runs me an imaginary bath in an enormous bathtub
that's big enough to swim in and it smells divine.
We cast off our imaginary clothes
as though they weren't really there and
jump slip dive slide into lemon, bergamot and lavender
steamy hot slippy bathtub and do somersaults
in the imaginary waterfall that he just invented where the taps are.

Sometimes it isn't all that easy,
sometimes I come home, and he isn't there,
he had a crisis at work, and he had to stay
because he's really important
and he comes to see me all het up about something,
then I have to calm him down with chocolate and red wine.
Sometimes both of us are too busy doing other really exciting things,
so, we don't have time to see each other.
But that's ok too.

And sometimes we argue ...
I get jealous and insecure because he's so wonderful
That sometimes I don't believe he really exists.
And we have an imaginary fight
and I tell him that if he really loved me, he would exist
but he says no it doesn't work like that ...
and he says that if I keep believing in him
then he'll never go away
and I'll never meet somebody who really does exist.
and I laugh and speak
well, I don't want somebody who really does exist anyway
because they don't always say the right thing,
and they can't make waterfalls appear in bathtubs.

And he says no, that's true but then some of them
do brave and powerful things,
Some of them are kind, compassionate and talented
and some of them are real.
And then I start to cry and speak
I wouldn't know what to do with something real
I would be too scared of losing it.
and he strokes my hair and says nothing
(he *always* knows the right thing to say!),
Then we curl up on the sofa and watch
stories about other people's imaginary lives.

Polly Walker

Porcelain Lady

Inspired by three Chinese plates in a glass case at the V&A Museum.

Pale pure porcelain lady
wound with delicate drapery.
Waves curl and curve around her, standing on the sand.
Foam encircled: seas surge rhythmically
against her perfectly balanced body.
Expressionless face, not a hair out of place
on her high-combed smooth dark head,
stillness amid disturbance.

Wait, she must wait for centuries, ages, forever
before he can reach her;
gallantly dashing through waters rising up to engulf him.
Speed of the steed and the rider bestriding.
Immense is his strength and the purpose that urges him forward.
The long lines of the waves and their curves
Straining against him,
his swiftness contends with their stresses
like tresses that stay him.
Scrolls rolling, controlling, delay him.
Aquamarine and terracotta,
faint black lines, delicately delineated.
Such surge of energy in so small a compass.

And she, standing serenely,
no seas can engulf her.
Safely she waits
in aquamarine and terracotta,
the delicate lines pile combers.
Feather foam sea spray spiralling
separate steadfast, forever.
There is a third person placed beside these two
not directly concerned.
In aquamarine and terracotta
he stands in arboreal contemplation
he may be responsible for the whole predicament.
He may have nothing to do with affair.
Over him, a tree spreads,
under him earth unrolls,
delicately delineated.
He is immersed in musings of importance
complacent, remote, self-sufficient.

Rachel Lister

Love Letter from an African Hotel Room

By the time you read this,
I'll be on a plane to somewhere warmer,
thinking about the way things used to be.
Wondering about Eve's apple tree
and the tyrany of choices forever offered to me.
But, I've been doubled up inside, trying to decide
wondering what's the purpose of a purpose-driven life, if I'm alone?

Baby, by the time you read this
I'll be on a plane to some old war zone,
wondering about the choices that I make.
What a rise it is to sacrifice - am I a broken warrior, a wounded healer?
Could I be helpful, could I be useful? Powerful or dutiful?
Oh, the world - I have to prove to you,
that everything I do for you - is all that I am worth
somehow, it's not enough …

> But it's not you, it's never been you.
> I know it doesn't ring true, for all the times that I've left you.
> It's not you, it's never been you.
> It's something that I have to do, keeps me from you.

Why is it some of us are born to luxury while others born into tragedy?
Just sit back relax and smile,
satisfy myself to sit and watch this on TV?
But that's not me… it's not me… it's not me….

> But it's you, and it's always been you
> how do I convince you, it's not enough?
> It's me, and it will always be me,
> it's something within me, burning deep.

By the time you read this,
I'll be lying awake in some African hotel room
thinking about the life I've left behind.
Suddenly your face in all those airport lines
comes running through my mind.
I think about your eyes, I think about your smile,
how tenderly you comfort me, and all the pain subsides,
I know it's love… But I don't know if it's enough
Then it grows, and suddenly I know:

> It's you, it's always been you.
> You're the one that I run to, the one that I come home to.
> It's you, it will always be you…
> Now, there's something I have to do and darling, it's you.

Polly Walker

I spent 18 years travelling frequently for work, particularly in Africa. I often wrote to an 'imaginary person' I might one day come home to. This song tries to capture being torn between your sense of purpose, and the need for home and love.

Widdershins

Why should one ever try to write anything?
Except to let the words run through one's fingers
Like ropes of sea-sand,
And hear the wind whistle between the verses –
Fruitless futility?
As if one walked alone along a dry shore
And hungered for the waves,
And sought the far horizon
for the taut gleam of their arrival,
And found nothing …
Nothing but the dry salt-caked sand,
Trodden and retrodden by millions of feet;
And yet no sound of life stirs in the sand,
Or whispers from the dunes behind,
Or from the clear sky
Where never gull nor diver
Smudges its dustless infinity:
All empty, swept, garnished and waiting –
For what strange tide, what terrible reversal
 of our eternity?

Rachel Lister

Scapa, 1945

Outwards we rush, the engines steady beat
Throbs in my eardrums like the boom of fate
Over the sea all ridged ad curled and neat.
In the blue sunlight, suddenly elate.
On the horizon sparks a diamond light -
Our target: diamond named and diamond bright:
Far distant still, we see it scintillate
At once and now it is a cruiser, great,
Grey, spiked and underneath us, sudden roar
And upward heave and now I feel the soar
Of gaining height, and as we turn to leave,
Once more it is a tiny speck of light
Far far behind, on the horizon bright.

Rachel Lister

The Transformation of a Winter Coat

A Cinderella story about the redemptive power of friendship between women.

When I arrived, she was secretly installed.
A frail and lost overcoat of a person
hanging in the wardrobe of someone else's life.
She wrapped them up on dark winter nights
when they had use of her.
They'd bought her cheap, brought her home,
then left her there to hang.
So, she just hung around waiting for another winter day
when she could feel needed.
Like an unloved second-hand store reject,
no longer in fashion, but equally warm.
With a history of being worn on winter days
and left in wardrobes when the sun was shining.
This frail and lost overcoat of a person
no longer knew the world as a warm and happy place.

And I? Well, I did nothing unusual.
I took her out, of someone else's wardrobe
brushed down the dust, remarking she was, after all, beautiful
I wore her outside - even when the sun was shining
stars were clear and birds were singing.
I wore her like a lavish cocktail attire
through decadent and sparkling nights.
Then and there, in a few deep breaths
she was transformed and found
that all along - she was not just a warm and shabby overcoat -
She was also a summer dress,
a satin evening gown of classic elegance,
a pair of light foot plimsolls, a playful rah-rah skirt,
a saucy strappy corset, and a well-loved snuggly jumper.

With that, she packed her over-stuffed trunks and left,
the wardrobe of someone else's life.
Knowing that one day
she will be an entire summer and winter wear
in the right place at the right time.
And I, left newly naked, as guileless, as the day I was born.

Polly Walker

Favourite Places (The Bookshop Song)

I want to wake up, Sunday morning
listening to Radio Four again.
Maybe I'll take a walk through Magdalen gardens,
maybe I'll …
Answer the bell, run down to the canal -
It's me and my bicycle, again and we
go to my favourite bookshop to see
touch and smell and breathe
thousands of pages that I will never read.
And I finally see, I finally see,
that my favourite places are things that you'll never see.

There's rain on the mountain,
I'm soaked to the skin and
I run past the old power station down to the cairn.
I go to my favourite hay barn -
it's my favourite hiding den.
I run from the breeze to the cover of trees
and oh, for the safety under the eaves …
I finally see, finally see
that my favourite places are things that you'll never see.

It's not why I came here again,
to tear you from your heart and your home and your kin,
but I don't know where else to begin.
I've got a lot of love for you,
a lot of life to live through,
a lot of world to show you,
and all this comes between me and you …

So, these are some of my favourite places
I think I'd like you to see.
These are some of my favourite people
I think I'd like you to meet.
And this is my favourite bookshop,
filled with books that we might someday read.

Polly Walker

Lesions of Love

Three times trauma struck
slicing neurons clean apart.
What fired together now re-wired:
love with pain, trust with hurt.

Once, a year of lies
revealed by a pocket call
confession of his thievery,
triumph at my delusionment.

Twice: A disappearance.
Six months my lover - now
a missing person. Grief was agony -
preferring death to mystery.

Thrice: Betrayal.
First a woman then a child.
A year they lay together, she bore his daughter.
He abandoned both, thinking only of himself.

Three times trauma struck
slicing neurons clean apart.
What fired together now rewired:
love with pain, trust with hurt.

Polly Walker

The Seven

A poem about a love bonded on the seven planes of existence.

In the first:
>I lie in your arms for hours
>enthralled at the perfection of fit.
>I eat and am sated by your calm strength.
>I drink and am quenched by the tenderness of your kiss.
>In your spreading warmth and healing hands
>I find myself – once warrior, protector,
>held inside a bastion of comfort that I do not wish to leave.

In the second:
>Released from sin, connections are completed
>through a simple act of fusion.
>Releasing bubbles of energy that fizz and pop
>as laughter, joy, and overwhelming love
>come bursting out of our tangled bodies.
>We know this is no illusion of our reptile minds.
>But in the night, bedtime will become bedrock
>on which to build a tower.

In the third:
>We've danced a long while in darkness, forwards and backwards.
>You've struggled and I've held you
>listened and consoled a complex flow of emotion
>wishing they would flow through me.
>But now they do, and I am the riverbed.
>I am the channel through which your torrential heart
>can pour itself wide open.

In the fourth:
>Capturing your imagination in that firelight
>divesting in you a stream of consciousness.
>You are the unwitting vessel for my entire life.
>You revel in these stories and listen, wide-eyed
>and I can feel myself alight before another glowing fireplace
>far from here in space and time.

In the fifth:
>Digging deeper, drawing at threads of our mutual philosophies,
>we weave them into braids, then ropes on which to climb.
>Deep beneath the surface layer, we mine
>each other's minds for that precious and rare stone:
>Implicit understanding, without analysing, questioning.
>Outlining the cosmic shape of things in darkness
>we emerge from there more golden.

In the sixth:
>To speak of the world and its exhausting consumption,
>we hold still the values that can put our hearts at peace.
>The rights and wrongs of destructive connections
>too weak and quick to satisfy our compunction.
>Moral indigestion settled, put at ease through faith,
>faith alone, but not religion,
>and this brings calm relief.

In the last:
>Something glimpsed from darkness into light -
>A tiny squint upon the far horizon.
>We are assured, as individual souls
>that sought and found sweet moments of unity with God,
>we might cautiously approach together.
>And in so, the binding of hands beneath another altar
>take a new communion in one another.
>Fusing then together all the seven,
>and enter then the light -
>at last, again, as one.

Polly Walker

for a better understanding of this poem, refer to Dion Fortune's "The Esoteric Philosophy of Love and Marriage", which articulates the occult belief in a true spiritual marriage being one in which two individuals are connected on all seven planes – physical, sexual, emotional, intellectual, philosophical, moral and spiritual. And that two souls bonded in The Seven, become one soul in death. I wrote this about my mother and father's marriage.

Fifth Age: Motherhood

Motherhood, a timeless and universal theme, encapsulates the essence of love, sacrifice, and resilience. It is a journey that transcends boundaries of time, culture, and circumstance, shaping the lives and identities of women in profound and multifaceted ways. In this chapter, we embark on a rich exploration of the theme of motherhood, delving into its complexities, joys, challenges, and transformative power. At its core, motherhood embodies the miracle of creation and the profound bond between parent and child. From the moment of conception, through the trials of pregnancy and childbirth, to the lifelong journey of nurturing and caregiving, the experience of motherhood unfolds as a sacred tapestry woven with threads of love, devotion, and selflessness.

Yet motherhood is far from linear or homogeneous. It encompasses a myriad of experiences, each unique and personal. For some, motherhood is a long-awaited dream fulfilled, a source of boundless joy and fulfilment. For others, it may be fraught with challenges, loss, or uncertainty. Moreover, motherhood extends beyond biological ties. Whether through birth, adoption, or fostering, the bond between a mother and child is rooted in unconditional love and commitment.

Yet, amidst the beauty and complexity of motherhood lie challenges and contradictions. The societal expectations and pressures placed on mothers to balance caregiving responsibilities with professional aspirations, personal fulfilment, and self-care can often feel overwhelming and unattainable. Moreover, the idealized portrayal of motherhood in media and popular culture can create unrealistic standards and feelings of inadequacy or guilt. Nevertheless, despite the challenges and complexities inherent in the journey of motherhood, it remains a source of profound growth, transformation, and empowerment for women around the world. Through the joys and sorrows, triumphs and tribulations, the theme of motherhood serves as a testament to the enduring power of love, resilience, and the unbreakable bond between parent and child. In this chapter we delve into the theme of motherhood, exploring its many facets, narratives, and implications for women.

Life Stirs in Me

Life stirs,
Deep in me
I have felt three times
This thing.
Now the years go on,
Old is my body.
No more is the cradle
Where they grew.
But now in them, life stirs
Deep they feel it
Over and over
Back in time
Forward in time
Rocks the cradle –
The womb of the world.
Women are
Fields for the plough.
Bright grows the seed
Harvest and then
On goes the tale.
Watch the young corn
Tend it and reap it.
Watching the reseeding
Over and over.
We are the earth,
Blind in our darkness
Grows the new life
Onwards and ever.
Deep in me
Life stirred
So, I once
Stirred in my mother.
Nothing is different
We must obey -
Follow the pattern
Of reproduction –
Oh, what are we doing?
What was left to Pandora?

Rachel Lister

Maiden to Mother: Waiting to be Rescued

Mother stuck in Maidenhood
with dreams of being rescued.
I waited for love,
I waited for 'him' to come
so I could start the life I had learned to imagine -
Father, mother, one to three children.
A pretty house in country.
Picnics under a tree.
Bike rides and campfires,
a real family.
He digs in the garden,
I bake in the kitchen -
But I waited for love
and love did not come.

Mother stuck in Maidenhood
with dreams of being rescued.
I waited for love
but love did not come.
What was I afraid of?
Taxes and mortgages
pensions, life admin
one-person holidays.
Fear that society had concluded:
table for one, not enough.
Single mum in her thirties,
not good enough.
So, I let go of dreaming,
in lieu of baselining -
Survive, struggle, juggle.
The years went by blindly whilst
I waited for love.

Maiden to Motherhood:
I stare at the bridge.
Till I heard a voice saying:
What if it's you now, just you and your daughter?
Accept it and go.
Then from a dream or a bubble,

we step forward: Me and my daughter.
Striding out boldly,
I carried her over the water.

Maiden now in Motherhood:
We live in that cottage
by a lush painted river
and soft willow tree.
We have bike rides and campfires,
moon-bathe from our lawn.
We dig our own garden,
cook spells in the kitchen.
My daughter, my dog,
my beautiful family
I waited for love -
and now true love has found me.

Polly Walker

The title is taken from an inspiring book called "From Maiden to Mother" by Sarah Durham Wilson, which articulates some of the archetypes and beliefs that hold us back from becoming our own woman. For me, on the back of a couple of decades of travelling, and being a single mum, I did think I 'needed' someone else to make my forever home. Thanks to an important conversation with my father, I was released from that fiction and had the courage to manifest it for myself and my child.

This Darling Drudgery

Let others see the words I wrote alone
and all the mystery is plucked and gone.
I take the pen and let it have its head
and watch it in idle wonder as it flows,
hoping to see a masterpiece unfold.
To exercise the mind, or let it run
unthinking as the midnight clock ticks on.
Out of my turmoil in this haven here,
where all is safety and domestic peace,
why is there such a devil of unrest
that fights to out and run and run and run
shouting aloud for freedom – and from what?
Freedom from care of children, care of house.
Freedom from love and kindness, and for what?
Better to live in this blissful slavery,
this darling drudgery, most excellent obscurity,
than find oneself outside in the cold world,
buffeted by the unkind winds of life
and only ones own worth to trade upon,
than learn how little value is your mind,
where should you find an ear to heed your voice
feebly expostulating.
Nothing learnt, so nothing to expound.

Rachel Lister

Russian Doll

I am three in one
and one in three,
whichever way you look.
Top layer all Babushka.
Grey-haired grandmother,
flat shoes and bus pass,
no head for gadgets or social media,
but full of what they call wisdom, hindsight and history,
guardian of family, keeper of ways,
nurturer, 'she who must be given a chair',
she who tells tales about the past, (and repeats them).
But she faces an uncertain future…

Uplift me, take me apart
and inside I am a young mother,
child on hip, pan at my elbow,
shoulder to cry on, feet on unsteady ground,
lover, mate, parent, initiate, juggler of all things,
yearning to fly the nest of my own making.
Then the middle years, as the newly adolescent
grow away, push away, pull you apart and leave.

Uplift me, take me apart
and I am that adolescent, the maiden,
withdrawn into my own dreams,
blushing at womanhood, uneasy in my skin,
rushing into young love, surging with sudden energies,
searching for self in the mirrors of fashion,
the 'who am I 'imponderable',
the learning of many facets.

And inside that is the indivisible child,
the essential being onto which the soul builds
in many shapes, layers, and disguises.
But here too, on either side is my mother, of potent memory,
and my daughter, of vital presence,
as many-layered as Russian dolls.
I lean on both, both lean on me.
I nurture both, both nurture me.
I am truly, deeply, one in three,
and three in one.

Mary Lister

Seismic Shifts – on PTSD

Such aching bones and scars
that run through me are
seismic rifts
from time to time that move and shift,
uplifting pain and painful memory alike
like silent movies watched
at night,
I lie -
I sleep to dream.

I see the haunted doctors come
I see myself crouched down
afraid but not afraid
detached and masked, immune.
At night I sleep
strangled by an unknown hand
and wake in other rooms.

My busy head on shell-shocked shoulders lay
embracing mind and spirit whole.
As sober fades the light of day,
and save for flesh,
and shards of shattered bone
find nothing left for me to cry upon
I sleep and dream
alone.

Polly Walker

For Motherhood Sake, Create

You fool! You hate the work that makes life go -
for husband, children – and it must be so;
The hand must sweep and dust and cook the food,
garments be washed, and dull things understood.
For better to live orderly and neat
than waste one's time in dreaming of the sweet
and perilous lure of beauty, half-defined
and strange desires and turmoil of the mind.
To wish to make and fashion for one's own
something of loveliness in book or stone:
Creation is for those who toil and think
and not for those who linger on the brink
of knowledge, in a lazy dream.
Complacent sippers of the vital stream
who to succeed must strip and plunge and fight
and after struggle, learn to swim aright.
Then mastering the current, deep in lore,
can hope to bring rich argosies ashore.
Creation – is it selfish or sublime
to weave another thread across all time?
For those who *care* to follow or reject
to pull to pieces, sneer, debunk, dissect?
No matter, you can never hope to swim
weighted by pots and pans, detergents, Vim,
the stove, the sink, the washing and the rest.
Your children and your husband are the best.
(If this is all the kind of stuff you do
the future will not miss it, nor will you).
Turn from your sterile brush, your unripe verse
in *true* creation all your art immerse.

Rachel Lister

Love is Freedom

Marriage takes feeling into legal custody.
How can love grow, where there is no equality?
Why should we corrupt the liberty of passion
incarcerate and deny its autonomy and freedom?
Not for me, possession.
My love will never be a prison.
My love should be a garden.
For he or she that walks in there,
would leave again,
more golden.

Polly Walker

Wide Open Spaces (The Sperm Bank Song)

On approaching thirty-three, it's a mystery to me
why everyone seems to be
more appealing than they ever used to be.
I know it's not my fault, it's just my body clock
And the gin is wearing thin, but my cellulite is not...
I don't know why I feel this way,
but I know I'm only an oven away from the bun.
Some say evolution's done us wrong but that's ok.

>I'll take the wide open, open spaces, empty places.
>I'll take the last ticket on the train, and I'll go my own way
>It's a small price to pay to be home again.

I've played the field I've played them all
and I'm getting rather bored
and I know I'm too fussy but can't afford to be.
Will someone smear my lipstick?
I'll never let the mud stick when
they leave you in the morning
without conscience, without warning.
Sitting at home watching Ally McBeal
ripping the clothes off a microwave meal,
bleaching my roots and waxing my thighs,
breaking my back for a piece of love pie - Not I!

>I'll take the wide-open, open spaces, empty places and
>I'll take my half-heartedness to extremes, follow my dreams
>though they're ripping at the seams, or so it seems.

Charlotte finds him at it again, it's driving her insane -
it's a small price to pay.
See how Margaret takes the blame when he beats her again -
is it a small price to pay?
Mr Right gets drunk again,
but is he boring? Is he lazy? Is he really worth the pain?

So, I do my dates in my dungarees.
Stephen King and Harry Potter, they're the only men for me.
One trip to the sperm bank, thank God I've only God to thank!
Then me and my sweet baby, think how happy we could be.

I'll take her to the wide open, open spaces, empty places
We'll be the last people left on the train, go our own way.
I'll be the last princess left on the shelf,
with no wedding bells for me
I'd rather love myself - It's better for my health.

Polly Walker

Written as a song in 2001, when there were various popular shows about women's battles with being single and finding a man: Bridget Jones, Sex and the City, Ally McBeal –intended in some way to be a depiction of career women and sexual liberation, yet the romantic endeavours of the characters are still undermining, through the myth that finding a man is the only route to happiness.

Nobody/The Invisible Woman

I wake in the morning, drink my two pints of coffee
wake up my children, time to take them to school.
Then I open my laptop I've got hundreds of emails
I've got dozens of meetings and that's how I'm spending my life.
Then I stare at my ceiling, I can't describe what I'm feeling
somehow, I have become this uncomfortably numb.

> I'm nobody. Nobody, nobody knows me
> part of a rat race of invisible lives.
> I'm nobody. Nobody, nobody knows me
> would anyone even notice if I just slipped out the side?

Then I get to the evening, and I turn on my TV
and I don't even watch it, I just stare into space.
In this little grey country with all its little grey people
automatic motor monsters
plastic disposable life.

> I'm nobody. Nobody, nobody knows me
> I'm part of a rat race of invisible lives
> I'm a living ghost. Mother, wife, and party host
> would anyone even notice if I just curled up and died?

Now I'm dreaming of mountains, I'm dreaming of airplanes
I run through the forest with the wind in my eyes
where the mango trees are swaying, and the children are playing.
Hear the radio chatter, imam calling to prayer
Here I am somebody, everyone, everyone knows me
across the Sahara, even the wind knows my name.
Where I am reclaimed, where I am somebody's soul mate
I walk to the sunset and all the colours just fade.

Then I open my laptop, I've got hundreds of emails
I've got dozens of meetings, and this is how I'm spending my life.

> I'm nobody.
> Nobody, nobody knows me
> I'm just a part of a rat race
> a plastic disposable life.

Polly Walker

A song about the experience of mothers as they 'disappear' to themselves in place of the functions they perform – at work, at home. Invisible Woman Syndrome is a legitimate concept for women in their 40s and onwards, linked to the division of labour in the home, juggling a career and childcare, identity and independence struggles.

I Did Everything Right, Didn't I?

On being everything the world wants 'her' to be.

I did everything right,
Didn't I, didn't I?
I proved myself worthy
Didn't I?

Mum's little helper
Daddy's sweet princess
I was such a good girl -
a moderate success.
Behaved like an angel,
I worked hard at school,
was average at tennis
I learned to act 'normal'.

> I did everything right,
> Didn't I, didn't I?
> I proved myself worthy
> Didn't I?

I was always polite
at those family functions.
Developed my faith,
my own thoughts and compunctions.
I got a degree,
then two and then three.
I travelled the world -
my compunctions and me.

> I did everything right,
> Didn't I, didn't I?
> I proved myself worthy
> Didn't I?

Hell bent on marriage
I dated relentlessly.
Got a house and some children,
excelling in normalcy.
I worked, played and socialised,
served school committees,

I mothered my husband,
worked hard to stay pretty.

> I did everything right,
> Didn't I, didn't I?
> I proved myself worthy
> Didn't I?

Those elderly aunties
still somehow look down at me.
I'm taken for granted
the bosom of family.
The burden is heavy,
the world's closing in on me,
I'm bleeding inside,
what more do they want from me?

From maiden to mother,
from woman to crone
something inside of me
frozen to stone
is searching and longing
and bursting with energy
ready to flay off
this flesh of society

If all women are free,
why collude to imprison me?
If it's still a Man's world
why do men want so much from me?
I'm humble! I'm grateful!
I'm all I'm supposed to be!
I did everything right.
Didn't I?

Polly Walker

Other Men's Thoughts

"But they were the notions of other men!" - Kipling

Other men's thoughts! How still they crowd
And throng and jostle, each to each
And this one softly, that one loud
They push my own thoughts out of reach
The beauty writ by other men
The glories of the running line
Surely, they cannot but condemn
These hopeless echoings of mine

Alas the race of verse is run
And naught is new beneath the sun
Or of course one can
Try anything to scan
Or not to scan
Just to be original
Or animal or vegetable
Indeed, to be
A modern poet
Can be
Quite
Easy
Just you
Try
IT

Rachel Lister

Hold Your Horses (A Song)

Have you ever noticed?
And if I told you, would you even show an interest?
Would you tell me it ain't true
that lately I've been talking in my sleep?
You never listen, but you always hear me.

I was waiting for a moment
to mention my apprehension.
I never chose one, and now
I've made my bed to lie in.
And lately I've been screaming in my dreams,
you never hear it but it always deafens me.

> So before… battle commences, hold your horses
> Tell me what's worth fighting for?
> Lay down your weapons, cast off your armour.
> You know it's not worth fighting for.

As I listen to you breathing, I feel my fear is healing.
But in the morning, the anger's back again.
Lately, you've been so cruel.
But that's not like you, so I take the blame for what you do.

> So before … battle commences, hold your horses
> Tell me what's worth fighting for?
> Lay down your weapons, cast off your armour.
> You know it's not worth fighting for.

So … come back … everything's forgiven -
I'm still the mother of your children.
Gone but not forgotten,
this battered love we've broken.
But lately, I've been sharpening my swords
I never draw them but then, all we need is words.

So, hold your horses
please don't charge what I've left unguarded,
I have no more defences.
Tell your forces that the battle's over
and the cause is not worth fighting for.

Polly Walker

Judith, by Klimt

She stares out at us, this Jewish Mona Lisa,
enigmatic, half in triumph, half surrender. Dulcissime!
Sex and death meet here.
She is Freud's golden woman,
challenging us in an uproar of textured facets,
like a shaman in a tranced vision,
holding a sacrifice to her breast.
She gazes at us through the dark future years of war.
She sees perhaps the rise and fall and fall again of Vienna,
the desolation of Europe, and two generations lost.

Grey flickering screens in staccato pointillism
pierce out the stuttering black images
of men fast marching into oblivion,
and Jews frogmarched from the Ringstrasse
into ghettoes, stamped with yellow stars.

But does she see beyond,
glowing and golden as she is,
to the murderous kilns of Belson and Auschwitz,
where dark glorious hair like hers lay in piles
for textile, wig and felt? Where soft supple skin was stretched for soft
glowing lampshades?
Does she see the Nazis requisition her,
possess her like a scalp, or Holofernes' head?
Own her? Sell her? - a trophy for the Art Market?
From Belle Epoque to desolation.

Does she see the colourless cold war years
of Third Man Vienna of brutal betrayals
in blackout alleyways, and the grim cycle
of the big wheel as it turned.
Does she smile through the long dark scream of Soviet times
with Europe, cut up like shoddy, in tatters, scattered?

But here she is, translated, all glorious colour, vital, alive.
This New Woman is new-born, in textured triumph,
challenging us through the woven layers of her future,
flirtatious, defiant.
"I am Life," she breathes.
"I am Woman. I am Art!"

Mary Lister

To Browning's Unknown Painter

Pictor Ignotius, how I feel with you!
For me, the pictures I will never paint,
for you, your endless "series, Virgin, Saint"
for each, the will, but not the power to do.

You feared the coldness of the world's survey
and I, the searing blast of critic's pen,
so, I like you, will shun the gaze of men
and write of what I choose, in my own way.

And like your fading frescoes' gentle death
my pages shall remain unread, unblamed,
as you preferred your dearest works unfamed.
So, I will write and risk no unkind breath.

This was the poem that inspired us to publish Rachel's poetry – your words will not go unread after all; we have made sure of it!

Sixth Age: Crone

Over time, the roles of women have woven themselves into a complex tapestry, rich with the experiences of girlhood, motherhood, and the profound wisdom of elderhood. In this chapter we explore the evolving identity of older women, casting off the dictionary-defined pejoratives, and embracing or re-embracing the figure of the crone from pre-Christian times, with a modern take.

Historically, the crone was a figure who was revered, misunderstood, and mythologised. Society viewed her with suspicion, particularly after the witch trials, when female power was so heavily suppressed, myths and stories evolved as propaganda devised to relegate the 'wise' older women to the shadows. The word itself—crone—has been marred by negative connotations, evoking images of malevolence and decay. Yet, this perception stands in stark contrast to the crone's origins in pre-Christian traditions, where she was revered as the wise woman, the elder, the midwife, and the healer. In those ancient times, the crone embodied the cycle of life, death, and rebirth, holding the knowledge of generations within her being (see the poem The Cailleach). She was the living repository of the community's history, a beacon of wisdom, and a guide through the mysteries of existence. In the archetype of the crone, we find the culmination of the divine feminine trinity—the girl, the woman, and the crone—each stage a vital part of the sacred cycle of life, the Triple Goddess who embodies creation, nurturing, and wisdom.

In writing this book, we wrestled with this term, searching for a word that captures the essence of the crone without derogation. However, nothing in our lexicon fully honours the depth of her role. Perhaps this struggle reflects a deeper societal discomfort with aging when it comes to women, and we see more and more with the expansion of plastic surgery, Botox, etc., pressure on women to *never* grow old (and yet somehow, we revere older men as 'Silver Foxes'). Scientific research supports the vital importance of these elder women. Studies suggest that the longer lifespan of women suggests an evolutionary advantage in reproduction – in other words, grandmothers contribute to the survival of their descendants. Neuroscience further reveals that the female brain undergoes an 'upgrade' after menopause, improving in areas related to cognitive function, emotional regulation, and wisdom once freed from the influence of our reproductive hormones.

This collection celebrates the often-overlooked contributions of grandmothers—women who have moved through the trials of youth and motherhood to become pillars of strength and reservoirs of knowledge. Grandmothers are the glue that binds families and communities, the keepers of traditions - an essential role to society as a whole. We hope these words inspire a reawakening to the value of the elder women, and appreciation for the crone that lives within us.

Reclaiming the Crone

We, the undersigned... present our case before the adjudicators of the Oxford English Dictionary, requesting the immediate withdrawal and replacement of the hideous debasing definition - a linguistic aberration, an insult to all women.

> Crone [krəʊn] *noun*
>
> Old woman, hag, harridan, fishwife, witch, ugly, evil, beaten and bent.

Who is this woman? A shrew, a gossip, a nag, a scold? Yet, we find no other term within your pages, to define a woman who is simply old! Replace this lexical carrion, with our rightful Crown.
Corona! Not Corogne! Referred to obliquely as "the power behind the throne" throughout the dark ages, now finally in the 21st century – we are hereby "Reclaiming the Crone."

We, the women of age, of senior years, through the change have now thrown off the mantle of gendered control. We are now ageing gracefully, with dignity, and wisdom. Can language capture us through the ages and stages? Beyond the change, no longer the vessel more the elixir, the pourer of blood to the next generation Carer, caregiver, grandmother and friend. Guardian of family and culture - Keeper of morals and wisdom, she midwives her knowledge - and harvests her experience. Old men, dodder through old age into insignificance, not us! We bounce through menopause with new zeal, passion and thrust! We've read Louann Brizendine and now know the truth; we've been set free from chemical slavery. We are upgraded! Wise woman, matriarch, sits now in glory, in her garden, beyond. Crone: sibyl, prophetess, seer, soothsayer, diviner, oracle, mystic. "The one who sees, more than with eyes alone, through the eyes of the psyche" - long-long sighted.

Here is our proposed alternative definition:

Crone: [krəʊn] *noun*:
- "An older woman, mature and unfettered by the demands of love and motherhood, who performs a vital role in society, culture and family."
- "A woman or womxn of wisdom and experience"
- "One who sees with her heart."

Mary & Polly

The Crone

In a quiet corner of the village,
sits an old woman with silver hair.
Her skin hangs loose, leather worn
by the Middle Eastern sun.
Her eyes, like pools of ancient lore,
hold the wisdom of memories, of decades.
Her face is a storybook, traced in lines
that tell of the wars she has seen,
mountains she climbed,
the children she carried.
Her hands, weathered by time,
hold power and life
from the babies they bathed
and the bread she kneaded
for each generation.

She sits now, peaceful, whispering secrets.
still and painted, in the noon-day sun.
The crone, keeper of the flame,
is a portrait manifest - power and grace.
I catch her eye and smile contentedly-
We know each other tacitly.
She and I are one.
And the crone in her speaks
to the crone that's
in me all along.

Polly Walker

Sit Beside Me (to Rachel Lister)

Sit here, sit there
and talk to me.
Tell me a story or two,
or one for every year I missed of you.
Flip with me through
the pages of each diary
and explain to me what it is you wrote
here and there,
which doodle what, and why?
Are they scribbled art of absent mind
or some yet deeper inspiration?
Flick old-movie-like through each loft-hidden album,
and who is who and where?
Confess: what you really did on the banks of Loch Ness,
and why were you dressed as Henry the Eighth that time?
Must I just let it slide?
So much seen, yet so much left to show,
so much lost, so much I'll never know,
unless you sit now with me and tell me so.

And come here,
just here beside me
and whispering that poetry
the ones you know
by heart and soul to me,
and quote-unquote me into
deep tranquillity.
Or just sit still and listen while I read
unfamiliar through the text,
stumbling unmetered I pause one second, less.
As you fill in the gaps it seems
they are words that speak themselves
and care not from whose lips they leap.
And let us wile away the afternoons this way
and armed with love, and tea
we winnow through the books in sheaves
until we're overcome with sleep.

Then lie
curled in sleepy eiderdown are you and I,
and in between us lies just fifty years.
Then sleep.
One-eyed, one-eared,
one hand to muffling radio hum
that never was white noise to me.
We drift in commentated dreams
until I hear the swish upon the landing
that measures out the night.
I save the deepest sleep till morning
creeps in dusty shafts of light.
We wake, I break
egg-like through my half-moon sleep
to sit, just sit, and chitter chat with you.
Cup-coffee smiles and morning kiss
of silky grey and soft old-lady skin.
This cushion comfort never-time,
this only Mousehill-Corner-thing,
where I'm always "mama's baba"
and you're always "fat white flipperling."
So, sit, sit there, sit here with me
and let's do it all again.

Polly Walker

Mitochondrial Ball

Who knows how I got to this ancient old hall
in the mysteries of history, a sacrosanct place.
The invitation said "Ancestral Ball -
You will dance with your forebears,
grandmothers and grand-mères,
and feast with your ancestors all face to face."

Attached to the invite, a pair of soft wings,
that flew me through mitochondrial lines.
I entered the doors of Unthinkable Things
and there before me innumerable hosts
of all my great-grandmothers, real - not just ghosts -
stretching right back to the earliest times.

Greeted by grandmas, such loving I felt!
I danced with them, talked to them long through the night.
Back through Victorians, Normans and Celt
to Neolith grandmother dressed in fur pelt.
We chatted till dawn rose with rosy first light.
I embraced them all, kissed them all, hugged them all tight.

For each of these women were part of a chain -
a mitochondrial female link,
repeated in essence again and again.
I am just part of some vast interplay
stretching through history to my life today,
and beyond my granddaughter, I think.

The band played a signal, and everything ceased.
The doors opened wide to a magical sound
for the latest guest at this sumptuous feast.
The bearers brought forth a small wooden throne,
on which was ensconced an ancient old crone,
then cheering and clapping was heard all around.

This Ancient of Ancients stood up tall and proud.
Her piercing blue eyes shone bright as twin stars.
She searched out for *me* in that great thronging crowd.
She summoned me up to the foot of her dais.

She held out her arms in a welcome embrace,
this greatest of all great grandmas.

"Oh, welcome my daughter to all of us here.
I am the first mother, the first Womankind.
Let all women everywhere love and revere
their mothers and daughters right down their line.
We are one indivisible, unbound by time.
One soul of one body, one Feminine Mind."

We all joined our hands in one great circle dance.
The orchestra played a new mystical song.
The hall echoed loud with our mesmerised chants.
The music we sang was the Music of Spheres,
down through our bloodline, through millions of years.
One Woman forever, *together* belong.

Mary Lister

The Mystic

There is a growing mystic within me
that in silence and prayer
raises its features against the glowing sun
and celebrates the interface of inward and outward blessings.

A soul torn open in a wave of ecstasy
cherishing the liquor of spirit
and dancing in the empirical moonlight.
All that is known, and distantly tangible
dangles like the stars above us.

A face turned upward in wonderment of
all that lies between the speckles of light.
Planets and stars: that which is physical and measurable
to human minds, a minute percentage of that which is knowable
is scattered between these aeons and lightyears of mysteries.

The merest counting of stars, a glimpse of eternity
tumbles upon me musically; wordlessly.
While education should filter from sense -
observation and only this, but the mystic within me
sees piercingly through all of this darkness
and cries out for joy and rapture for all that is not seen.

Polly Walker

How to Have Your Midlife-Crisis

Start limbering up on the sidelines.
Get a feel for how it is done.
Your stupendously wild mid-life crisis
when you can go mad and have fun.

First the Botox, and lipo-sucked buttocks,
a nip and a tuck here and there.
Then let rip with embarrassing garments,
and outrageously dyed purple hair.

Try to embarrass your children.
Spend weekends with lovers in Nice.
Drive a very unsuitable sportscar,
and flick V signs at traffic police.

Go for lap-dancing in Rio,
yacht with bankers in San Tropez,
blow all your pension in Vegas,
and wherever you go, Seize the Day!

Learn to become more eccentric.
Leave hotels without paying the bill.
If your children object to your lifestyle
just cut them out of your will.

When you've mastered these minor adjustments,
pull out all the stops and surprises -
Stage a splendid and beautiful climax
to your well-earned and wild Midlife Crisis!
(because '*You're Worth It ...*')

Mary Lister

A Mermaid Comes Out on Her 60th Birthday

I'm coming out of the closet,
and revealing to you my all.
I was really a mermaid all along,
not a real woman at all.

I've been hiding my secrets completely.
For years I've secluded my tail
in a very large, oversized handbag,
suspiciously shaped like a whale.

So complete were my cunning disguises,
no surprises or clues all those years
(except doing the breaststroke round Sainsbury's
and fish floating out of my ears.)

I'm the very last mermaid in Yorkshire,
but under this M & S vest,
there's an ocean of passion and seaweed,
and a seashell clapped onto each breast.

Now they say no one does love a fairy
who's approaching some forty-odd years.
Try being a mermaid at sixty,
it drives one to drink and to tears.

The Council's just written to ban me.
They say that my singing's a joke.
My alluring songs are like clashing gongs,
and my siren sounds more like a croak.

So now that I'm finally 'outed',
I'll not stay to sit every night,
pointlessly wailing alluring old songs
with never a sailor in sight.

I'm off to the wild open seascapes,
to the heaving blue waves and sea spray.
And I'll swim with my ancient old mariner -
our future is turquoise, not grey!

So, farewell to pretence and illusion,
this mermaid, though long in the tooth,
turns her back on the waterless wilderness years
and recovers the dreams of her youth!

Mary Lister

My Grandmother's Hands

You were far too picturesque to be true,
brushing your fountain of long white hair every morning
with a tortoiseshell brush in each hand,
hoisting it loosely into an angel-white bun with long pins.
With those same hands, you gathered your skirts
and waded knee-deep in the river
to cut watercress for the W.I. stall in Cirencester.
The garden was your golden Cotswold kingdom:
Great borders with lilies, peonies,
crown imperials, lavender and cowslips.
You taught me their names, as I trailed behind you,
with my toy wooden barrow,
to the herb garden, with its drowsy light-headed smells
of marjoram and lemon-mint,
that you planted with those same hands.
It was a green world, a child's secret place.
I dreamt green dreams poured from your hands.

Impossibly beautiful too,
the nightly bedtime requests for piano playing.
Warm and fresh from our baths,
we would hang out of the bedroom window,
listening to you playing the piano below –
Chopin, Schubert, and Handel, rising like swans
into the moon-spun twilight.
Hands, those hands again, dancing over the keys
releasing music into the dreamy evening air,
taking me far beyond childhood
to the sweet sadness of humanity.

In sepia prints those hands held reins of horses in India,
watched over by turbaned men -
Drove antediluvian cars, shook hands with men in plus-fours,
waved handkerchiefs from castle windows.
They held, kid-gloved, a wedding bouquet.
Those hands clasped my father,
dressed like a doll, as though he might break,
Or pushed him in a pram shaped like a galleon.
A distant pre-war gracious world, forever in sepia tones.

A century later I found a key that fitted your little treasure chest,
a carved inlaid Portuguese box.
With trembling hands, I opened the lid,
and found, like a minor Tutankhamun hoard,
photos of lost brothers, medals, your silver glasses case,
wedding photos ... How beautiful you looked, impossibly beautiful!
And there, at the bottom, a pair of perfectly tiny white kid gloves -
your wedding gloves, child-sized and delicate.
I remembered those hands, brushing hair, planting herbs,
playing Schubert....and they reached out to me
palpable and real, they touched my cheek,
those soft kid-gloved hands.
A presence, a being.
Not just an impossibly picturesque memory
of an impossibly picturesque grandmother.
To me, beautiful.

Mary Lister, about Hermione Lister

The Window

I remember a window long ago
opening out on a summer evening
on to a garden of peonies and lavender.
My sister and I leant out to listen
to our grandmother, white-haired and beautiful,
playing Chopin in the room downstairs,
pouring the sounds from her rippling hands
out into the vibrant evening air -
music sent and received through windows.
And when we slept, we dreamed
in chords and arpeggios of liquid light.

Mary Lister

Rage

Written with Yeats's Old Men in mind.

Rage used to be exclusive to old age,
and Trolls were ancient mythic things
that turned to stone in the primeval dawn
if caught by the first glimmer of light
before the distant age of Viking kings.

Now new trolls stalk the twilit earth,
raging text-obscenities into spaces,
poisoning the cyberworld with verbal blows.
The old stare fixedly in rows
with stony resignation on their faces.

And Road Rage trundles the highways of the land
frustration fans the pandemic fiery mood,
fury's the zeitgeist of the age of Me-First.
Jealous entitlement's insane outburst
fragments a world where life might still be good.

The Old sit placidly on buses.
They mustn't grumble, mustn't rock the boat.
They have their pensions, mustn't make a fuss.
Now it's the Young that rage…and rage at us!
It's youth that now grabs Old Age by the throat.

Mary Lister

My Muse's Ashes

What vast uncharted oceans reach before me?
Of knowledge without end and deathless story
Of the world's wealth of man's created glory!
How can I hope to know in my short day?
One-millionth particle of this array?
(And here I look with loathing on the page
At this inadequate and trite verbiage)
Oh, added torment to my lack of worth.
To know enough to feel my own sad dearth.
Of any spark of genius divine!
Ah, give me even one quite perfect line,
And let the rest go, (as indeed they will)
To feed tomorrow's hearth or as a spill
To light my husband's pipe, while he, poor sweet,
Stamps out my muses' ashes with his feet.

Rachel Lister

To a Modern Sculptor

And must we worship gods of steel and wire?
All angles, blocks and hopeless twisted forms
Writhing in torture that they cannot feel
To expiate the whole world's guiltiness
Of sins committed and sins yet to come,
Atomic outrages, the bitter knell
Of this brief dynasty of *care* and calm?
"It is The Age" you cry "of Thinking Man,
Have done with milksop maudlin imagery
Of naturalistic form, and pious art
That glorifies a non-existent God,
To spoon-feed those whose minds cannot aspire
To that great *plane* of dispassionate thought
Where we may dwell amid our abstract shapes
And rule as Gods supreme upon the earth."

Superior intellect, this may be true,
And had the creative impulse thought as you
You might have looked like one of those things too!

Rachel Lister

Villainous Villanelle

An old man sitting on a gate
Disconsolate and quite alone
I wonder why he's out so late?

The moon shines down upon his pate
It gleams away like polished bone
An old man sitting on a gate.

He thinks of days when he was great
And influential and well-known
I wonder why he's out so late?

Perhaps his watch has stopped at eight?
He gazes at the grass new sown,
An old man sitting on a gate.

He's musing sadly on his fate.
And now and then he gives a groan
I wonder why he's out so late?

The moon sinks down at such a rate
And still, as motionless as stone
An old man sitting on a gate
I wonder why he's out so late?

Rachel Lister

The Cailleach

The wind howls at the frost moon's wane
from Samhain's wake, now the Hag's abroad.
Painting snow in mistral curls,
tumbling, squalling, powder-like ashes from her cane.

Old woman, mist-veiled on her mountain throne.
From Ben Churach to Ben Nevis, she flies,
her hammer splintering rock, renting valleys,
slicing fissures in our bones.
She wails in grief like Banshee, even the Fae-men groan.

Beara, Queen of Winter, hails her advent
dropping rocks and earthquakes from her wicker basket -
leaving ancient wisdom, cairns and ley lines.
She screeches, one-eyed, blue-faced, red-toothed,
atoning brutal winter with her dark lament

The Cailleach's call breaks our own wounds open wide.
Not bleeding, but freezing, cold to the bone.
When she cries, her wolves will answer.
When she calls, the storm hags fly by
to wash her plaid in coastal whirlpools,
laying long, white shawls of snow across the darkening tide.

Crone moon, the shadowed face of Brighde
weaves a craft that's feared, unknown.
It is she, Dark Goddess, that knows me of old.
And those who bury their faces in the dark night of a winter soul.
upon her bones and shoulders, all our troubles laid.

Against her rasping braids, I've climbed up relentlessly.
Where I am knocked down, I've gotten up,
forbearance, tolerance, tenacity.
Digging deep to call a cold and inner stillness
the Cailleach, on this hostile ground, steers and comforts me.

My body full of bitterness, my blood is cold and sweet.
A heart as strong as Gallowglass, I fear no death.
I will hold fast to the last sheaf of harvest,
with warmth embrace the spinster's fate.
And in her arms, we overwinter, she bathes my hands and feet.

Beneath the holly, wait in stone till comes the Wild Hunt
when Brigid's fire, in spring reborn, she's healed and young again.
Frost abated; splinters freed, all bitterness is gone.
"When we lived, dear mother, it was the people that we loved." *

Polly Walker

*A quote from the folk song "The Cailleach"

Life Without Breath

Over me flows
Life without breath
Under me goes
Sleep without death
Dreams of joy
Unfading are
Unlit my lamp
Lightless my star

Waiting alway
Power to come
Bursting to say
Yet ever dumb
How shall I know?
What I will be
When with the rush of spring waters
The tide will return to the sea.

Rachel Lister

My Mother, Rachel

She wasn't just a mother, a nurturer. She was a huge soul.
She was our culture, our humour, our history, our language.
From her DNA we inherited some of her body and half our minds.
But from her memes, her core, her heart, we inherited
our whole way of being.
Her playfulness, joy in life, imagination, conjuring up Scottishness -
Singing songs to us children, dancing with knickers on her head to amuse us,
reciting poetry from memory, drawing Tolkien's trolls,
and William Morris maidens, stories of mad ancestors,
of haunted castles, and Celtic beasties.

Stories too of the War, and her stint in the Orkneys,
shifting ships with a long paddle for Scapa flow manoeuvres,
her life as Chelsea art student, the romance of meeting our father
washing his socks in the bath with his feet.
Love at first sight, a prerequisite of true love.
The daring tale of conceiving me on the night train to Bad Honningen
and my sister on the shores of Loch Ness.
But my little sister appeared at a window, tapping to be let in.
All told as if we were legends, not at all immaculately conceived…
Above all, her intense love of art, of literature, of myth itself.
Of history and culture all around us. Our zest, our core, our comfort
all inherited and passed on to three daughters.

We never knew, as tousled-haired toddlers,
How we flattened her dreams, *Art Interruptus.*
How could we guess she felt a poet manque,
Drowned in nappies, ground down by the grind of family?
Yet we became her singers, dancers, poets and artists,
and passed her legacy on to our own tousled toddlers in turn.
Like a giant relay race, take it, run with it, pass it on before you go.

You were more than a mother, darling Rachel, mother, grandmother.
You were a whole way of life and living.
A vision with ever-open arms and smiling face.
May I be this to my own children and grandchildren,
to my daughter and granddaughter …
Open arms, smiling face, big heart, huge soul.

Mary Lister

Seventh Age: Death

As we move into the final chapter of life, we enter the seventh age—death. This is not merely an end, but a transition, a moment of transformation that touches every generation in its wake. In this chapter, we explore the role many of us play in the care of the elderly during their final months and years, and the significance this holds for grandmothers, mothers, and granddaughters alike.

For the crone, this stage is both a return and a preparation. As she approaches death, she begins to revert to a childlike state, relying more heavily on the care and support of those around her. In this vulnerable phase, the crone sheds the burdens of her past, distilling her life's wisdom into stories, memories, and quiet moments of connection. She imparts these gifts to her family, leaving behind a legacy of knowledge and love. For the mother, this is a time of emotional complexity. As she cares for her own mother, facing the impending reality of loss, preparing to feel alone in a way she has never known previously. Whilst deeply painful, this also serves as a rite of passage, stepping into the role of matriarch her mother leaves behind, filled with doubt about her ability to do that. In this transition, the mother learns to navigate the space between holding on and letting go, balancing the needs of her dying mother with her own process of mourning and growth. For the granddaughter, this is often her first encounter with the death of someone close. It is a formative experience, learning about the cycle of life and death, forcing her to question where her grandmother has gone, and what happens on the other side.

In caring for Rachel at the end of her life, we witnessed this dance between life and death - sorrow and love with moments of unexpected magic, which we have tried to convey. This time of caregiving is a sacred exchange, where the crone prepares to depart, the mother takes up her new role, and the granddaughter learns deep lessons of mortality. Each facing death in their own way, yet united in love. In this chapter, we address the delicate subject of death not as a loss, but as a transformation. In the seventh age, the crone's transition becomes a gateway to the next cycle, reminding us that in every ending, there is also a beginning.

The Mother Ghost

If I died now, I think I would return
on still summer nights to my garden.
I'd wander out from darkness quietly up the path,
and stop to stroke the ghosts of my two cats
as they sit sunning themselves in the moonlight.
If you looked out, you'd see the pale glow of my dress,
and hear me humming softly, preoccupied with gathering
flowers out of the vibrant night
for some vase in the hushed gloom of a cold church.
But when the winds blow from the moors,
and rain lashes the trees against the house,
or fierce November howls beneath the doors,
you'll see me pressed against the windowpane
with blazing eyes and streaming hair,
calling to see my children once again.
Fists noiseless on the glass,
cries voiceless in the storm.
Then let me in, please let me in,
and welcome home the cruelly exiled ghost!

Mary Lister

Lingers (the Unquiet Grave)

Softly falls the winter night
lands heavy on my shoulders.
Why do you look so surprised, did you notice how time passes?
Patiently the firelight pours between my fingers and I say
"*Move closer. Stay a little longer.*
The touch of your skin beneath my fingers
how it lingers, it lingers."

Let's take a walk out to the woods
and build snowmen in the pines
tell me why do you look so surprised as
snowdrifts cloud my eyes up?
I can't feel your body heat and
I wonder where you are and I say
"*Move closer. Stand a little nearer.*
The smell of you in your old mittens
how it lingers, it lingers."

Suddenly I'm all alone and weather beaten hearted
I run my hands across the stone
wish it were me, departed.
Why do you look so surprised I can't move on without you?
I need you closer, to see your face a little clearer
to feel your hair between my fingers
how love lingers, love lingers.

When twelve months were gone
your voice spoke deep inside me.
It said, "*I'm sorry, though I loved you so*
I must leave you behind me.
As you grow old, I'll bless your soul with further love to find.
But now, you must move onwards,
life is full of wonders
I'll warm your hands through every winter
love lingers, love lingers.
So, when you feel the chill, know, love lingers still."

Polly Walker

Most British folk artists have covered the Unquiet Grave but have remained reasonably faithful to the original. Having no audience, there are no rules, I wanted to incorporate the intimacy of the parted lovers in the song, and the sense of loss.

The Mother-Daughter Turning Point

When was the Turning Point?
When did I cease to be daughter,
and became your parent?
At what point did you let me cook for you,
serve you? Bath you, and dry you tenderly with a soft towel?
Or read to you in bed, poetry and stories in the sleepless early hours?
Was it perhaps those visits to hospital?
Were they the first signs, the lit-up warning lights?

Or was all this just the forerunner
before all your goodbyes to everyone, but me,
round your deathbed scene, with all the family,
touching and so poignant with cards
strung like bunting for your birthday?
Then finally…finally, with deliberate finality,
You said, "I love you, Mary. I love you so much."
And let me go.
So, I was your daughter once more.

Mary Lister

Bedtime Stories

Back then, we walked together
through dark forests of stories,
and I protected her from wolves with teeth, and toothless hags
that rode *"In the night, in the howling storm."**
We laughed at the trolls, and marvelled at the fae-ness of fairies
The witches and wizards were incompetent.
We hacked joyfully through the rose briers of stories.
We sang songs and put nightmares to sleep.

Now she is more Mother to me,
helping me through impenetrable digital jungles,
alerting me to trolls in ether forests,
guiding me through virtual wastelands.
But maybe I have become the hag now myself,
decrepit, elderly, savvy not wise.
The only witches have weird kingdoms called 'social media',
and the wizards are scammers and hackers,
who make figures disappear … into their bank accounts.

The nightmares don't go to bed.
We are sleepless and fearful.
The stories loom large and come true.
We sit by the fire, but the dark spirits ride the skies,
cackling and claiming me as theirs,
a toothless chorus of whisperers.
Mother and daughter must hold hands again
and follow the path through dark times,
snatching at breadcrumbs.
The ending may not be happy …

Mary Lister

*A quote from The Sick Rose, by William Blake.

The Cypress Fading

The silver of the olive turns to green,
The dark flame of the cypress *glitters* deep
And the Italian beauty I have seen
Eludes the memory I strive to keep:
The mists of Apennine softly shading
The quiet colours when the day is fading.

And yet within my mind some fragments lie: -
San Miniato, green and grey and cold
In dimness glowed the altar, while on high
The ceiling blazed with bright mosaic gold.
From panes of marble, Topaz light was plying
On a black cross where the white Christ hung dying.

Evening, and San Gimignano, old and brown
Where time has lingered idly as in jest
Though half her towers have crumbled and gone down
And all who built them long laid to rest
Yet the dying daylight shades are streaming
Through narrow streets with swords and armour gleaming.

In Via del Colonna is a door
Through which one passes to a world apart
In utter silence stands enthralled before
The Passion, passionless, transcending art
The lovely landscape lies in peace profound
Earth holds her breath; the still *group* makes no sound.

How could they fail to paint their *loving* things
Where light falls with such tenderness and grace
And piety gives truth to angels' wings
And finds perfection in the virgin's face
Humble and high, above all women sainted
They worshipped and believed and thus they painted.

And yet their age was never one of peace
Their smaller world was far less safe than ours.
Our fear is universal, life may cease,
But death walked daily in that town of flowers
Blood waters genius well; and from much shedding
Beauty and learning grew, over all Europe spreading.

Rachel Lister

Glass

Wandering through an old junk shop I spied
a bell-jar, with a hummingbird inside.
I lifted up the glass. The bird began to hum,
"Oh, there you are at last! I knew you'd come.
Now follow where I fly without a word".
Speechless I hovered upwards with the bird.
A silver mirror hung dusty in the darkened hall,
and from within we heard a soft voice call.

"Only poets and singers may ever pass
into the bright world of the Looking Glass."
"I am a humming singer, she, a dabbler with words."
"Then enter!" said the sweetest voice I ever heard.
The mirror seemed to melt, and through the ornate door
we flew, into a magic world I thought I'd dreamt of once before …
A garden stretching far beyond our sight,
From dazzling daylight into starry night.

"Here you must find your life-long task,
Somewhere hidden in this garden in a cask.
I, the Silver Spirit, will be your guide.
Mirrored lakes and glassy woodlands, treasures hide!"
Listeners, how can I ever hope to tell or sing
the strange translucent quality of everything?
The mirrored mazes, glassy trees and crystal plants,
branches and leaves all shimmering in a tinkling dance.

How long we searched I never could recall.
At last, we found a jewelled casket hidden in a diamante wall.
Inside, "Your task is to return and use your voice
to show that every living person has a choice
to use each moment, savour every breath,
because Life is a miracle, beyond that, only Death."
But sadly, as I travelled home,
returned the hummingbird beneath the dome,

My mind fogged over, crinkled like shattered glass.
and I forgot my journey…and worse still, forgot my vital task.
Can writers not remember what to write?
It is our job to set the world alight!

Mary Lister

Two Dreams About My Mother

When my mother was in the final stages of cancer, I had two memorable dreams, which in their own way, helped us both to understand or at least accept death.

My mother had asked me to go out and buy her a beautiful white Victorian nightie to be buried in because she hated how the undertakers had dressed my father in a pale blue funeral 'uniform'. So, I performed this sad task and found a lovely white night dress with simple embroidered butterflies on the front. Then, a little later I dreamt that I was following a pale figure across the common where they lived, into the churchyard. It was my mother in her new white gown moving like a sleepwalker.

As I got closer, I saw her slowly lie herself down on my father's grave. He had died 10 months before. I was crying because she put her hands over her breast, like a funereal statue on a marble grave. I put out my hand to pull her gently back up to her feet, saying "No my darling one. No. Not yet. It isn't time." I felt, in my dream, an infinite sadness, as though she was my child, not my mother, and I had to lead her gently away because she wanted just to go quickly to him. But I had to tell her the simple truth that there were no shortcuts and that I was leading her back to face a long and painful illness because that was the natural way of things. She accepted like a child, took my hand and followed me. I cannot describe the desolation I felt that I had to lead her away from her 'shortcut' to a peaceful death. But it was the truth.

When I told her about this dream as she lay in the hospice, she murmured, "Yes! That is right. It's so true. That's exactly it! That is how it is." We discussed how sometimes dreams can send a simple stark image, that can both clarify and comfort.

Another dream I had at that time, was that my father, though I knew he was dead, walked in through the back door into the kitchen just like he always had, from the garden. He was completely vivid and alive to me. He said, "Now don't forget to tell Mum that she has an appointment on Friday. She must meet me at 10.45 on the green at Elstead (the next village to where they lived) I'll be waiting."

As I recounted this dream to my mother, we realised the meaning or significance. Elstead was where their dentist lived. Death was no more than an appointment, and my father had let her know that he would be there with her to help her through it. I can't tell you how much this meant to her, the thought that my father was saying in his usual brusque way, that he would be waiting for her at an appointed time, and how simple that would be. We were both atheists, and it was strange that at the point of death, we should get comfort from such a very simple image. She certainly did. But she died, not on the Friday, but on the Saturday, at exactly 10.45.

Mary Lister

It's Gone: The Inner Landscape of Dementia

I was once in this place ... where was it now?
Things weren't so blurred then,
there were timetables and special days.
There were gardens with little walls ... apple tree games.
People talked with you and not at you ...
I remember once ... no ... it's gone ...
A kind woman who held my hand,
and I had pigtails and a smocked dress.
Who was it once kissed me?
No, it's misted up ... I felt it, but it's ... gone.

I am here now,
Walled up in my own country.
The walls are indistinct and jigsawed.
A hand comes at me with a plate
and a sudden noise of clapping startles me,
from a black box that never opens.
Boxes open, don't they?

That reminds me ... no, it's ... gone...
There was music, a sort of song.
I can dance to it, arms in the air
suspended as I am in slow swirling ether,
the colour of lavender.
I can smell the lavender ...
I tap my feet, but the melody drifts apart,
un-focusses, disintegrates
just when I almost touched it ... it's gone.

There was a man, with a loving voice
who held me ... No... No ... he's gone ...
A flickering black-and-white world
where we kissed, and he said ... something ...
something ... gone ...
I almost grasped it, but it's ... gone.

"Get your hands off me!"
"Let me go!"
Rough hands pin me down.
I am bustled up in a white nappy, legs forced apart.

Someone says, "Calm down Freda!"
But they aren't kind, I can tell.
I shout to those outside the wall,
they are sitting in chairs, the blank staring women.
But they are gone, quite … gone.
There was somebody.
There was something ...
But it's… gone.
It's gone.

Mary Lister

Luckily my mother did not have dementia, but I wanted to explore this theme as so many elderly do and I wanted to explore what this may feel like.

Forgetting Self, A Villanelle on Dementia

I AM, but who I am, I have forgot,
and all my yesterdays have wandered far away.
I've lost my memory. I've lost the plot ...

I have forgotten who I am or what ...
Even what year it is, what month, or day.
I am... But who I am, I have forgot.

I have some childhood memories of play.
My mother held me in her arms a lot.
...Who was that man who touched me yesterday?

Of middle age, I can't recall one jot...
A *tabula rasa* ... glimpses that won't stay.
I ... am. But who I am ... I have ... forgot.

A missing person! Is it me...or not?
Shadow-misted memories gone astray.
All my yesterdays ... have wandered ... far away ...

Behind, the road is dark. Ahead the sky is shot
with brilliant stars in a dazzling array.
I AM...but WHO I am, I have ... forgot.
But my *tomorrows* beckon me ... away ...

Mary Lister

Fear No More

Fear no more fear of fear itself –
howling at midnight, startling from sleep,
hand gripping the gun, whisper of threat,
crack of the footstep at your back,
earth-pounding thud of exploding bomb,
the heart that beats
and stops at dawn.
You stood up and were counted.
I listened, watched and heard it all.

Peace now settles on your bones,
silent and secure in the deep soil,
full fathom deep,
and now in sleep the transmutation comes,
mortal and magical.
Unscreaming nights of subterranean stars
light up your endless dream,
and like a subtle flame, ignite some hope in ours.

Mary Lister

Inspired by Shakespeare's song, in The Tempest

Listening to the Light

Gentle voice of peace
touched my arm,
guiding homeward.
I listened for you.
Once swathed in shadows
crushed by night.
In bright dawn arose
a hopeful seeker.

Polly Walker

The Sleep Demon

Sleep slinks in the shadows,
whispering cold breath on fogged glass.
Calling my name in hushed, eerie tones.
Creeping and curling its fingers,
beckoning me to the void.
Days blur into nights.
A carousel of weary cycles,
where the hours stretch like elastic,
pulling me back, pressing me down.

In the dark, the sleep demon's eye-shine
glints back with hunger,
devouring my energy, dragging me under.
Exhaustion clings, a second skin
drapes a heavy cloak around me.
The bed beckons, an altar of my weariness,
where sleep is a thief of moments,
a silencer of life.

My dreams are distorted echoes
of a past I cannot grasp.
I am tethered to the thin edge of consciousness,
struggling against the insidious call,
to keep a grip on the waking world.
In the night, the air is heavy
with the weight of unfulfilled promises,
restlessly rolling as plans, and
ambitions slip through my fingers.

Yet, within the shroud of fatigue,
an ember glows with hope
that soon the Deep Sleep will come gently,
and I will rest.

Polly Walker

Skipping Stones

Our life is like the skipping of a stone
Sent by a cunning hand across a pool
Twice or three times it touches, water-borne
Then sinks and disappears, drops down alone
Into the darkness and dimness cool
Pity the stone that leaves the light forlorn,
Pity the soul that leaves the world, unborn
Again, into an element unknown -
For the body darkness, for the soul renewal.

Rachel Lister

The Carbon Cycle

Some wishful part of me had set out on a voyage,
and was dashed against rocks of reason.
There, my body cut its losses
and cast these shipwrecked thoughts adrift.
For I had been visited by a terrifying dream
that some strangled shadows of myself
might be weaved into the braids of time
and make *no impact* on their mottled hue,
but twist, entangled in the shades of blue:
of lives and secret histories that past
beneath the amber glow of fate.
Lit briefly and then burnt into the light
swept as ashes out into the careless night.
And there, dispersed as dust into the wind
settle and are buried in the furrowed brows of nature
overlain, impacted below where life begins anew.

If not my selfish spirit, then might my flesh feel comfort
in the endless renewal of all things?
Should not my hands rejoice that someday they,
might stretch out as the fingers of a tree?
Or my feet that they might storm a riverbed in wet stampede?
Might my heart not feel relief that it could become the sun?
And my blood to fuel the furnace of a blazing star,
can I not rest in peace, knowing we all will supernova?
If so, how should my body stomach
such gutless dreamings that my mind perverts
when we are all destined to be greater
than the sum of all our parts?

Polly Walker

Pass on a Little of What You Have Gleaned

Pass on what little you have gleaned,
Some love of beauty, joy in English words
Teaching the newly opened eyes to see
Earlier and more clearly
So perhaps they may sooner grasp
The freedom and the dream
And work out something for themselves from it
For one cannot live only on dreams of wonder and beauty
Especially when one's whole life is in reality
The stuff of the best dream of all, and a blessing indeed
For which I am humbly grateful – married love

Rachel Lister

Bound Wings

I wake from airborne dreams
and crash-land into a flightless body,
legs that tremble, tire too soon.
A mind alive with hopes and plans
caged by leaden flesh and bone.

I am seen, but do they see the
invisible chains that bind my feet?
Struggling to lift, to stand, to move
in a world designed for the unbound
fighting a force I cannot prove.

The earth moves faster than my feet.
And I, watch from the edge,
a bird with wings that will not fly.
In the world's commotion, I'm losing pace.
Yet inside, at night, I rise.

Until I leave this cage of bones
my spirit flies beyond its hold
and soars relieved from binds of flesh.
Although the sky is no longer mine to touch,
I carry its vastness in my chest.

Polly Walker

Child of Your Child – The Night is Behind Us

Strong words spoken, soft to my ears
the poet's candle lightens the weight of the years.
So ebb and flow the tide of the words
soothes my spirit, with every verse.

Write me kindly into a page of your heart,
rhyme and scan me cleverly such as your art.
Each Keats and Kipling and Tennyson verse
are said in your voice, and it's your fingers flow through the words.

> I'm child of your child, and you're Lady Shallot
> and I'm child of your child and I'm your butterfly
> The poetry you have made, are words that will never fade.

Paint me softly, bring me to life.
Watch me closely, watercolour me in light.
Every Rossetti and every Millais
you look over my shoulder, and the memories replay.

I'll sketch you lightly, wrap you up in shades of grey.
Trace you, blend you, fix you that you'll never fade.
Deep shades of you are etched in my heart
they flood me with light and lift me out of the dark.

> I'm child of your child, and you're Lady Shallot
> and I'm child of your child and I'm your Botticelli.
> the paintings that we have made, their colours can never fade.

I'm just a part of a masterpiece that you created
and the deep shades of green in me
are colours that you have painted.
Now that you're leaving, I wonder if I'm going to break,
but your poetry speaks to me and tells me I too must create.

So, I'll take the towel down, wrap it around.
Hug you, rock you, tenderly powder you down.
The night is behind us, there's no need to fear.
The storm will not wake us.
Curl at thy ease, my dear.

Polly Walker

As a baby, my grandmother recited Kipling's White Seal as she wrapped me in a towel. As a girl, she introduced me to Tennyson, Keats, pre-Raphaelites, and would paint me in the lazy afternoons together. I wrote this in the hospice thinking of those Kipling words "The night is behind us, there's no need to fear... safe in the arms of the slow swinging sea."

Death is a Garden

We think of the dead as beyond and above us:
Not so.
Eternity is alongside us, not distant and menacing,
but a garden outside the house that we live in
into which we will presently step,
shutting the door behind us …

Rachel Lister

Suggestions for writers and groups

We all have vivid memories, some strange, funny, or dreadful about each of these seven stages from childhood to old age. In this book, we have tried to cover some of these important transitions and the love, joy, and suffering that shaped our evolution. We've tried to show in the book how the different experiences we have as a child, woman, and old person (including across the generations) can be a rich ground for writers. If you would like to explore your own experiences through poetry and stories, here are some suggestions to get you thinking. Although this book is about women, these prompts might equally apply to men.

Quick-fire warm-ups for groups or in pairs

- What did you most love about your mother (or daughter) and what were your points of conflict?

- What was your relationship with your grandmother/s and how did that contrast with that of your mother?

- How does your generation and culture define the expectations of your gender?

- Can you describe the thread of connection through the generations in your family?

Writing prompts and inspiration

- **Transitions.** Choose one life transition and write some brief immediate impressions or memories. Can you make a poem or story exploring what changed, what was lost or gained?
    - *Inspirations: The Changeling, Kintsugi, Change – A Story, Mother-Daughter Turning Point, Maiden to Mother, Bedtime Stories.*
- **Reminiscence.** Write a tribute to your mother or grandmother in verse or prose. Was she perfect, loving, a rock, or was she chaotic

and wayward? How did your relationship develop from child to teenager to woman? What was her legacy to you?
  - *Inspirations: My Mother Rachel, Sit Beside Me, Child of Your Child, Drawing in the Dark.*

- **Childhood memories.** Looking back, what were you like as a child? Explore a memory that encapsulates your unique personality and the essence of you that remains.
  - *Inspiration: Russian Doll, School Fat, Mummy I Think I'm a Witch, Toddler Queen, Princess with no Knickers, Box of Delights.*

- **Transformation.** What are the transformative experiences that have shaped you as a woman, man or other? What scars or strengths have they left behind?
  - *Inspiration: Stillness, Learned in Loss, Bound Wings, Forged in Fire, Lesions of Love, Seismic Shifts.*

- **Generation and gender.** What are the parameters of gender that your culture and generation have imposed upon you? Did your aspirations conflict with those and how did that affect you?
  - *Inspiration: Girl in a Veil, I Did Everything Right Didn't I, Maiden to Mother, This Darling Drudgery, The Negative Committee, Nobody/The Invisible Woman, Love Letter from an African Hotel Room, Other Men's Thoughts, Questing Soul, My Muse's Ashes, To an Unknown Painter.*

- **Love.** Can you capture some of your most romantic moments? How did the shape and feeling of love change from youth to older age?
  - *Inspiration: Fair Knights, Warning Signs, The Click, Something Between, Wild Wounded Bear, The Link, On the You Beside Me, Love is Freedom.*

- **Birth, Death and Spirituality**. Explore through story, those unexplainable moments of intuition or connection to family, particularly during key life events like births or deaths. Delve into the idea that women might share a transgenerational spiritual bond.
  - *Inspirations: Dreaming of Her, Daughters of Copper Woman, Once, One World Many Voices, Life Stirs in Me, Mitochondrial Ball, Carbon Cycle, Death is a Garden.*

Printed in Great Britain
by Amazon